M000200793

LEADING PEOPLE IN CHANGE

Hero, an imprint of
Legend Times Group Ltd, 51 Gower Street, London, WC1E 6HJ
hero@hero-press.com | www.hero-press.com

© Jennifer Bryan 2021
The right of the above author to be identified as the author of this work has been asserted in accordance with the Copyright, Designs and Patents Act 1988. British Library Cataloguing in Publication Data available.

Print ISBN: 9781800316881
Ebook ISBN: 9781800316898
Set in Times. Printing managed by Jellyfish Solutions Ltd

All characters, other than those clearly in the public domain, and place names, other than those well-established such as towns and cities, are fictitious and any resemblance is purely coincidental.

All rights reserved. No part of this publication may be reproduced, stored in or introduced into a retrieval system, or transmitted, in any form, or by any means electronic, mechanical, photocopying, recording or otherwise, without the prior permission of the publisher. Any person who commits any unauthorised act in relation to this publication may be liable to criminal prosecution and civil claims for damages.

LEADING
PEOPLE
IN
CHANGE

A PRACTICAL GUIDE

JENNIFER BRYAN

CONTENTS

FOREWORD

JENNIFER BRYAN AND STEVE WELLS

The world is increasingly subject to significant change, and while the focus is often on the potential implications of exponential technology developments like artificial intelligence, robotics, adaptive manufacturing, augmented and virtual reality for example, political, economic, and social change are also happening at break-neck speed. This range of future forces – together with the current pandemic – act on life, society and business and add to our personal and organisational sense of complexity and uncertainty.

In the past, we have been confident in our predictions about how the external environment is evolving and been able to come to consensus about the way ahead. Increasingly we are far from certain about how the outside world is evolving and are less able to reach consensus about how to proceed. It's this situation that we believe calls for a new focus to leading change in organizations, and that's not easy. There's a temptation to always do what we've always done. But then we get what we've always got; except the reality is that the world moves on and we risk being left behind.

Change management is about people, and this statement of the obvious too often gets lost in over-complicated methodologies and technology-focused approaches to change. Leaders get seduced by the glitter of the gizmo and forget to pay attention to the ordinary, everyday needs of the people who will make the technology sing. Typically the people side of change is an afterthought, and noticed only once things are not working as planned.

With the current environment especially, a number of questions arise concerning the nature of change and the human face of change. There needs to be a new mindset to accept and embrace exponential change, to do so with more than an eye on plausible multiple technology-centric futures, and enable a more human-centric future.

Are we building a change programme that takes us towards a single, perhaps preferred future, or to help us prepare for a number of potentially different futures? Building flexibility, agility and resilience into change programmes by exploring plausible visions and situations is crucial for the future growth of our enterprises and the wellbeing of employees.

Using the ABChange Model in the context of these different potential futures enables leaders to generate a pathway that includes the people and ensures they are taken along this journey of change.

This approach ensures an organisation's 'greatest asset' is paid proper attention to, whether changes are seen as radical or incremental. It marries the person and the change task together in the different future scenarios.

Many leaders find leading people through change intimidating because there are emotions involved, sometimes difficult conversations, and it takes people out of their comfort zones. With the current environment, we have all been very much outside our comfort zones for a whole variety of reasons. So, bringing together two frameworks that enables us to plot out plausible futures and how we can lead in future, gives leaders the ability to really focus on the priorities for the business not just to survive but to generate growth.

LEADING PEOPLE IN CHANGE

A PRACTICAL GUIDE

INTRODUCTION

Change management is not rocket science; it is about people. Despite this, so many organizations go to great efforts to plan the logistics and practicalities of change without considering its impact on people. This can be for a number of reasons, such as budgetary constraints, lack of process understanding or lack of experience of the impact change will have on people – the list goes on. Typically, the people side of change is an afterthought, usually realized once the change is not working. In order to manage change successfully, consideration of the way people understand and deal with change is critical. This also enables managers to understand more fully how change will affect the organization as a whole.

I have worked with over thirty different organizations in both the private and public sectors over the course of twenty years. Every change programme has been different and I have been involved with each programme at a different stage. However, I have found one constant – people are afraid of the people side of change.

Several years ago, I was coaching a number of senior leaders within an organization, and at one point, nearly all of them said to me, 'Jennifer, I know about Kotter and some other theories on change, but what the heck do I do with this thing on my desk?' I decided when I was embarking on my Masters dissertation that I wanted to create a practical model that managers could use to answer this question. So, I spent a year drafting and conducting research to align two popular models, one in leadership and the other in change management – thus creating the ABChange model. The name of the model is very personal to me. I have child **A** (Amelia) and child **B** (Blake) and they **Changed** my world, as you can imagine.

I envisage this book will be relevant to managers of all levels within organizations that need to lead people through a specific change. The book aims to be a practical guide that demonstrates good practice, so managers can follow the model and lead people through change effectively and successfully.

The ABChange model has been applied in a range of different sectors, industries and organizations. The book includes a number of case studies that show how this tool has impacted various change programmes and projects. There are examples of the positive, as well as the detrimental impacts that can occur when the ABChange model is not utilized correctly. All of these case studies have been gathered through my consulting work with different organizations. The following chapters share some of the good, the bad and the ugly examples of change management and aim to take the fear out of the people side of change.

INTRODUCTION

My ethos is that there cannot be any learning without change, and no change without learning. I believe the two disciplines are inextricably linked, and hence to effect real adoption of change people need to be taken on a journey of change rather than to a destination. That is the intention of this book – to take us all on a journey.

CHAPTER 1

Isn't Change Management Simply Good Communication?

One thing is certain… change is all around us and is always happening because the world is constantly changing (Dawson 1996; Fullen 2001; Mabey and Mayon-White 1993). The big motivator for change is to make things better in one way or another (whether this is because of a crisis, high performance, reconciliation, market fluctuations, etc.). The specific reasons vary, but the overarching aim for organizations is predominately the same – to make things better (whether this is to increase profit, market share, differentiation, etc.). The desire for us as a society at the moment to make things better is enormous – all you have to do is visit the very large self-help section of any bookshop (online or otherwise). We are constantly looking to others to show us how we can be better than we are now – for example, by losing weight, or controlling stress or anger or… you can fill in the blank with a range of self-improvements. Our desire for improvement extends to our professional lives and the organizations in which we work. In these instances, the overarching driver for change or improvement is leadership. Statistics have proven that the most common reason an individual would leave or remain within an organization is due to the relationship, or lack thereof, with their line manager.

THE COMPONENTS OF CHANGE MANAGEMENT

So, how does leadership impact change? To start, let's discuss what change is and how it happens. At its most basic, change is what happens when you move from one state to another state (Lewin 1935). It is not a perfect process and cannot always be planned. Even when change is managed, it does not always go according to plan. A range of factors such as circumstances, finances and people can impact how change occurs. The way people react to change has a great impact, not only on the approach or levels of resistance to change, but also on whether the change is actually applied and happens. Taking into consideration that some people cope with unpredictability better than others, it is critical for managers to remember, first and foremost, the people they are leading and managing. After all, they are the people who will actually make the change happen, one way or another.

The way change happens is very dependent on the behaviour of people. As a result, there will be a strong focus on the behaviour of leadership in this book, as it is through behaviour we can understand what we should or should not do as leaders in change.

When it comes to organizational change or change within an organization, there is a dependency on the skill and ability of leaders to flex their leadership styles. For example, Sally was a senior leader in a regional office and her natural leadership style was coaching. When she first started out in the role, she wanted to change the culture of how her team contributed to and resolved business challenges – she wanted them to take more responsibility and collaborate as a team. In the beginning, her coaching leadership style was not enabling the change she wanted to make. This was due to the team not being used to working in this way, and they were sceptical of her motives and approach. The previous leader used a telling or commanding approach, so they were used to someone telling them what to do, not asking them what they thought they should do. Sally realized she needed to flex her typical style to help the team make the transition and demonstrate that she genuinely wanted their thoughts and ideas. It took some time, and took longer than Sally originally anticipated for the change to happen, but she eventually got the impact and results she was aiming for with the culture change.

Organizational leaders need to recognize that change is complex (Fullen 2001), imperfect and dependent on human behaviours. Managing change also requires flexibility in leadership styles. Many managers believe that if they tell people what the change is, then people will come and do/use it. However, experience has demonstrated on multiple occasions that this is not the case. People need to be brought along on the journey of change; they need to understand not only what the change is, but how different the new state is in comparison to the current state, and how that specifically has an impact on them – not to mention why they should cooperate with the change in the first place.

Individual behaviour has a great impact on the outputs of change, and it only really happens when people are willing to make the change. To continue the above example, if Sally carried on applying her typical leadership style of coaching, rather than flexing her approach and using different styles to help her team through the change, then she would not have achieved the results she was aiming for. This is because she needed to help the people in her team to change their behaviour and want to make the change. She needed to be confident and reassure her team that there would not be negative repercussions – her ask of the team was genuine and wanted. The role of the team in understanding and dealing with the change was critical to managing the shift towards a better culture.

Peters (1991) says we should not discuss change but organizational revolution. Argyris (1985) talks about change management as flawed advice. Kotter (1995) puts forward a top-down change transformation process; and Beer, Eisenstat and Spector (1990) discuss a bottom-up process. With all these different ideas on managing change, it is no wonder the subject is confusing.

So, perhaps the best way to start is to take into consideration the different approaches to managing change. If the view that organizations are complex open social systems is accepted, then those systems will impact the results of change within organizations

(Katz and Kahn 1966). As we have already mentioned, it is well known that change only really happens within an organization if the individuals are willing to make the change. The Congruence Model of Organizational Behaviour (Nadler and Tushman 1979) defines a set of four inputs that lead to a transformation process within the organizational components, which then lead to the outputs of change highlighted by organizational performance (see Figure 1).

Figure 1: The Congruence Model of Organizational Behaviour

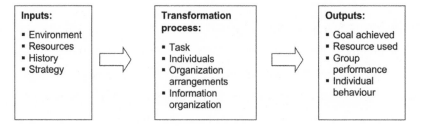

Source: Nadler and Tushman 1979.

According to this model, essentially an organization takes inputs and then generates outputs, so it is within the transformation process where change occurs. It is during this phase that leadership behaviours and skills are critical to the outputs generated. 'To change anything requires the cooperation and consent of the groups and individuals who make up an organization, for it is only through their behaviour that an organization can change' (Burnes 2004, p. 267).

The question is, how can leadership and change skills be linked together to give managers a roadmap to follow when implementing change?

Utilizing the model above, there are some key questions that should be asked at the start, when working with, managing or dealing with a change:

1. Who needs to be involved?
2. What tactics or methods will best deliver the change?
3. How ready is the organization and its people for change?

In my experience, the first two questions are typically asked within an organization, which is why stakeholder management and communication are two key elements within any change management job description. However, the third question – how ready is the organization and its people for the change? – is one that is not asked very often and can have huge impacts on the success of the change. It may seem obvious, but it is a common mistake within an organization for a person to decide a change needs to happen and pull together a project team without asking whether the organization ready for it. For example, do they have all the right processes, procedures, policies, tools to enable the change? If the organization is set up for the change, do the employees have everything they need? How ready are the people? – do they want to change? What is in it for them to change? Why would they want to make the change? Many times, the 'What's in it for me?' (WIFM) question is posed at a much later state in the change process, when actually it needs to be factored in at the very start of the change, as this will drive the vision, communication, motivation and hence the people through the change.

All of these questions should be used and asked by every leader or manager of change. This will help greatly when it comes to applying the ABChange model and driving the change down a path of success.

CHANGE MANAGEMENT VERSUS GOOD COMMUNICATION

Rightly or wrongly, experience has shown that many people believe change management is the same as good communication. In reality, they are very different disciplines. Communication allows people to know what is going on, when and where; in other words, it shares information. However, change, as discussed earlier, is about moving something from one state to another. Although communicating and communications are key tools within change management and help with enabling change, the sum of communications is not change. An organization can send out hundreds of communications about a project, but that does not equate to change, successful or otherwise. For example, an infrastructure organization was embarking on a digital change – they wanted (like many other companies) to be digital by default.

When they started the change, they sent out multiple communications announcing the change and the aim of the organization, but one year later, people still did not know what the change was all about, much less what they needed to do differently. Something more needed to happen to actually enable change to happen.

It stands to reason the business of managing change has a number of key steps and the articulation of these steps varies slightly depending on who is setting them. Stebbins (2017) argues that the quality of communication is the 'single most important contributor to managing resistance to change'. So, what makes a good communication and how does that contribute to successful change management?

There can be times during a project when it seems like the 'right hand does not know what the left hand is doing'. This is a clear sign that there is a gap in communication. When there is a need to move people from one state to another, clear and concise communication is critical to counteract resistance, as well as rumours, misperceptions and misconceptions.

Communication is a science and a fine art. The science is built all around the purpose: to give people information on what, where, why, how and when. However the fine art to communicating involves the elements beyond the logistics. The timing, tone, methods and channels also all play a crucial role in communication. If the communication for a change is too early or too late, then it will miss the mark and not have the desired impact, begging the question, why do it in the first place? It is the same for the other 'art' elements.

On a particular project with a financial services organization, there was a great deal of frustration, confusion and even anger within the project team. The reason for this predominately came down to poor communication. To combat this, communication needs to be clear, concise, authentic and genuine in what and how it comes across (Juneja 2018), which is how the situation was rectified. It was agreed what communication would happen, when and by whom, and if this was not completed for some reason, then the reasons for this failure were communicated. This tactic reduced the level of frustration and confusion within the project.

Communication also needs to be in an accepted form that fits the culture of the organization. For example, if an organization does not promote using email to communicate with staff, then that method would not be the best way for people to receive information. (More on culture is discussed in Chapter 6.) Several different types of medium should be given serious consideration to ensure an appeal to a wide audience (video, posters, emails, newsletters, etc.). Knowing how staff receive other organizational information is a good indicator of the best methods for communicating change programmes as well. The content itself needs to align with the company's cultural norms – essentially this makes it easier for people to receive, accept and process the information.

In order to influence stakeholders there needs to be a series of steps that enable people to reach different processing levels in change. The Kübler-Ross model (1969) defines these steps clearly.

From a communication perspective, it is about moving people through the change curve from awareness to understanding to acceptance and finally commitment. The space between understanding and acceptance is at the dip in the change curve, and there is a risk that people go around and around in the dip – what I call the 'washing-machine cycle'. To prevent this from happening, leaders and managers within an organization need to clearly build and express their skills in leadership, change and influencing by using good communication with their teams. The process of this should be integrated into the change and communication plan, in order to have a positive impact and help bring people along the journey of change. This will also help manage expectations and ensure people are given the right information, in the right way, at the right time. When change and communication are not properly planned, then the consequences can lead to high levels of resistance and potential failure of the change itself.

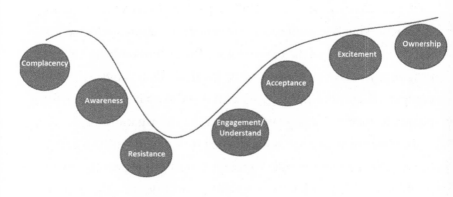

Kübler-Ross model (1969)

To provide an example, a central government department was bringing all its agencies together from multiple sites into one new building. The purpose was to have a workspace ready for the future and increase the level of collaboration across the agencies. This move would involve a total of 3,000 employees, utilizing not only different working styles, but also different systems and processes. The aim was to implement agile working and achieve a desk ratio to people of 1:1.2, in order to accommodate all the staff. The main issues were that the project team was not visible to the staff; neither the staff nor the managers were engaged or aware of the requirements of the change or what the project team would need them to do; and the agencies' offices were across multiple buildings in central London, making collaboration or sharing of any information challenging.

Unfortunately, a change solution was not put in place, or at least not one that was visible. Communications for the new arrangements went out to the agencies and staff affected only one month prior to the actual move. There was no consultation involved and staff and managers were left to make assumptions. There was also no mechanism for staff or managers to raise questions and obtain answers. Ultimately this had a detrimental impact on the change. There were high levels of resistance, which continued for years after the implementation. This was regardless of the new building and workspace being of a much higher quality, improving the working conditions and experience of staff overall.

KEY POINTS

- Change is dependent on human behaviours, so leaders need to think about how their individual team members cope with change.

- An ability to flex leadership style is important in order to enable change.

- Leaders should explain the reasons for change in a way that will ensure their team understands the purpose, reasoning, direction, objectives and impacts.

- Before making a change, it is important the right procedures, processes, policies, systems, tools and teams are in place.

- People within the organization who will be affected by a change should be given time to digest the information and ask questions. Leaders should be open to feedback.

- Leaders must ask themselves 'how ready is the organization and people for change?' and analyse the results before acting.

- Clear, concise, authentic and genuine communications can counteract resistance, misconceptions and misperceptions.

- The timing, tone and method of communication should be reviewed, as well as the information itself.

REFLECTIVE QUESTIONS

- What is your typical leadership style? What might you need to do differently, more of, or less of when leading your team through a change?

- Think of a change you are trying to implement at work. Why would your team want this change? What is driving and will drive this change – in other words, why do you need to do it and why now?

CHAPTER 2

The Role of Leadership in Change Management

'Sponsorship is the number one
success factor for change.'
(Creasey and Hiatt 2012)

So many organizations, in my experience, have not realized the importance of leadership and sponsorship in implementing change. They are critical and without them change simply won't happen.

However, one could argue that all change programmes have a sponsor and leader at the front – that is how the budget was approved, after all. Why is it, then, that some change programmes are not successful, or at least not nearly as successful as they could have been? In my opinion, these cases occur because the sponsorship and leadership is not correct. For example, the change was not led by the right person, was not done in the right way or was not committed to fully – there are a number of reasons. So, what or rather who is the right person to sponsor and lead change?

Well, to begin with, we need to separate the two elements slightly. The sponsor of the change needs to be someone highly influential within the organization – someone who can build and encourage a network of other highly influential individuals to provide the ownership, responsibility and resources that enable the change to happen – in other words, someone who is active and visible. More often than not, the best person for this role is the chief executive officer (CEO) or managing director (MD) of the company. This is because it is those individuals who can influence the rest of the board to support and take responsibility to ensure the change happens within their respective areas, and hence across all the different business areas in the organization.

Now you may think, 'That is very far reaching and surely not all change programmes need such high-profile involvement?' And you are correct; however, if you are trying to make a truly organizational transition, then, I would argue, yes, it needs high-profile sponsorship to ensure people sit up and listen. On the other hand, if you are looking to change the structure of your team or the team's way of working, that may not require the CEO of the organization to sponsor it per se, but it will require the board member who is responsible for that area to support the change and communicate this to the rest of the members. Therefore, in that instance, you would need the board member of the business area to be the sponsor.

This may come as a surprise to you, but I would strongly encourage you to give sponsorship of your change some genuine consideration. Consider what you would need to make a restructure of your own team happen: you might need a different budget or budget allocation, and new job descriptions created and applied, and hence the cooperation and collaboration of the human resources (HR) department. You might also need to promote the new structure and ways of working to other business areas and teams, not to mention the fact that the reason you are implementing a restructure most probably is due to a change in team function or focus. All of these things hence require support from wider business units and teams and therefore you need an executive sponsor to help pave the way for change.

For example, I once worked with an infrastructure company on a digital transformation. This transformation impacted the whole organization, across the globe, and required a completely different set of behaviours from all staff – from how they interacted with clients to how they performed for clients, what they performed, and how they interacted with each other through communications, processes and systems. The sponsor for this change was the MD with strong support from the chairman. This was critical, as the transformation required everyone, from the board, executive and senior leadership all the way down to graduate level staff to change how they worked. Without this level of sponsorship, there was no way people would have not only felt they had the permission to change, but allocated the resources required to make the changes.

One of the changes within this transformation was creating a new operating model that would bring all the processes and systems into one place. Prior to this, all the processes and systems used by different teams were hosted in a number of different places, generating confusion, miscommunication and frustration across the business units. There were multiple anecdotes of individuals feeling it was 'pot luck' if they found the system they needed. They would usually end up asking several people before finding it, and then would save it in their favourites so they did not have to go through the process again.

A team was created to review how a new operating model could be developed and created that would make it easy for staff and leaders alike to find the processes and systems they needed to get their work done. A team of individuals from different areas of the business was formed, including those with technology, change and branding expertise. The project required their time, knowledge and organization to create this completely new operating model. If the overarching change, which this new model was a part of, did not have the full sponsorship of the MD, it would have been extremely difficult to get the resources required to make this happen, if not impossible. It took the team several months to develop a model, agree a language/words for the categories within the model so people would know how it use it. Then there was another month of working with different team to test the model with groups of staff located across different regions, levels and digital or technological capabilities.

Testing with staff in a cross-section of roles and regions was critical to ensuring the model would work for the whole organization, which also helped the executive sponsor and project team with obtaining full buy-in from the rest of the board before the launch. The model was also compared to other similar models in the marketplace to help illustrate its use and impact. Due to this great level of investment, the model was successfully launched with extremely minimal negative impact – in fact, I can share with you: there was a total of five people out of 16,500 who phoned and complained they could not find a certain system they were looking for. (In these cases, it was then explained to the individual that, for example, the finance system they were looking for was located in the 'Finance grouping'…) Executive sponsorship was absolutely critical to obtaining the level of investment and commitment to create, develop, test and launch this new operating model. Without it, the resources would not have been made available because the drive and importance would not have been emphasized, and hence the adoption rate would not have been so high and seamless.

Likewise, I was working with a different client on a digital transformation programme, and unfortunately we did not have executive sponsorship, or any real sponsorship within the organization. As a result, the change was driven by the IT department and hence implemented as an IT change. This had quite a lot of detrimental impacts, because as stated earlier, change is about people, not rocket science or IT, or HR or finance, or whatever business unit is implementing change. This transformation also required a number of behavioural changes from staff in terms of how they communicated and interacted with processes and systems, both between themselves and with their clients. However, without the executive sponsorship there were a number of challenges the project team encountered: people not having the permission or time to read the communications, complete the actions required, participate in the training or access any post-transformation support.

All of these challenges could easily have been overcome, or avoided completely, with the right sponsorship within the organization. However, without that sponsorship, they became huge obstacles that stopped the change from happening, or resulted in resistance from staff. All of this contributed to an increase in the time for adoption and decreased the level/extent of how they adopted the change, which had a major impact on the financial cost and performance of the transformation.

The importance of the right sponsorship in order to ensure change is adopted and has an impact cannot be stressed enough; there is a direct correlation between the effectiveness and engagement of the sponsor and the success of the change (Festinger 1954).

To embed change, there needs to be a high level of enthusiasm from the people who will be implementing the change, not just the team overseeing the project. Obviously the project team need to be enthusiastic, but to a degree that engenders enthusiasm in others. This happens by creating a positive momentum with the whole change network – the executive sponsor, then the managers, project team and champions should work side by side with the key stakeholders by coaching, listening and helping them through the change.

At the end of the day, change is a journey… a story. The question is: how do you want to travel and what story do you want to share?

For example, while John Swain is actually credited with the invention of the lightbulb, many people believe it was Thomas Edison. In actual fact, Edison did not invent the lightbulb, but he did figure out a way to mass-produce it. If we think of Swain and Edison as leaders or managers of change, which one was the most successful? The one who invented this world-changing technology or the one who took the technology and made it possible for people to use or implement it? The fact we typically think of Edison as the inventor goes to show that influencing others to change is when we really do have great success. We need to bring people along with us on the journey, help them with the change – just doing it ourselves does not have nearly the same impact.

THE RELATIONSHIP BETWEEN SPONSORSHIP AND LEADERSHIP IN CHANGE

Now you may be wondering, 'OK, I get the sponsorship element but what does this have to do with leadership?' I would argue: everything! How one leads influences how leaders communicate, hear and interpret messages, along with their teams, and whether they undertake the necessary actions. For example, my daughter, even as a very young baby, would not do things unless she knew why. If an authoritative figure said, 'Don't touch that!', she would look at you and either do that anyway or ask the question, 'Why?' If she did not have that information, then the chances of her complying were extremely slim – this is still the case today. And to be fair, this is very much like a good many of us. We have a strong desire to know the 'why', but we also need to be told, asked, persuaded, influenced and coached – in other words the messages, including the 'why', need to be communicated to us in a way we are willing to accept them. This is entirely down to leadership and leadership styles.

USING AN ORGANIZATIONAL DEVELOPMENT APPROACH TO CHANGE

The first question a leader needs to ask themselves when leading a change is: 'What kind of change is this?' Referring back to the model in the previous chapter by Nadler and Tushman (1979), a leader needs to know what is at stake for the organization and its people in relation to the change. To understand what type of change we are dealing with, we need to know how ready the organization and its people are for the change. It can be helpful to take an 'organizational development' approach to change (see Figure 2) and build up a picture of the situation by asking people from across the organization to answer questions, such as the following:

Figure 2: An organizational development approach

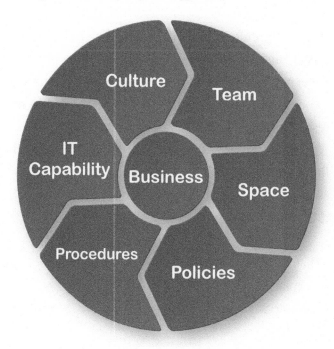

BUSINESS

- What is the current and future business strategy and model?
- Why does this change need to happen now?
- What is driving this change?
- Who should be the executive sponsor and why?
- How will the buy-in and commitment of the executive sponsor be obtained?
- What is the organization's commitment level to this change?

CULTURE

- What is the culture of the organization – will it help or hinder this change? If both, then how and why?
- What has happened historically within the organization during the past three years? Has it just gone through a number of restructures, growth or other changes?
- As a result, what is the mood of the people? Will they want this change, or will they be sceptical, or both and why?

SPACE

- What is the environment like to enable this change in the workplace?
- Is remote working going to be used more, so fewer desks are needed?
- Do people need remote-working equipment in spaces outside the office?
- Does more collaboration space need to be developed?
- Will the current space help or hinder the change?

TEAM

- Is there a team of people that already exists that can deliver the change along with what they already do, or does a new team need to be developed?

- How will this team be structured, what are the critical roles and at what level do they need to operate?
- What other support networks need to be in place for the change to happen? Does a change champion or agent network need to be established? If so, how, who and with what structure and support (regarding training, budget, etc.)?
- What is the structure of the organization and how are deliverables are completed? Will this support or hinder the change?

POLICIES AND PROCEDURES

- Is support from other business areas required?
- Across what period of time does this change need to be adopted? If there are systems, processes and teams that need to be developed, what impact will that have on the time and the budget?
- Will the existing systems and processes help or hinder the change?
- Is there a budget to support this? If not, then what needs to happen to get a budget and how will this impact on timings?

IT CAPABILITY

- What are the current IT and HR systems and processes – will they support or hinder the change?
- Do some changes need to happen with those systems and

processes first before embarking on this change, or can they happen in tandem, after, or not at all?

- If the change requires other supporting business areas to make changes (i.e., IT or HR) then does the vision of this change need to widen to incorporate them? And hence will this require a high level of sponsorship?

This list of questions is not exhaustive, and you may come up with others on your own, but you need to make sure you consider all the above areas when you are identifying the type of change you are looking to deliver.

Furthermore, time is a factor that is often overlooked with change. As a society, we have got so used to things happening immediately that we typically underestimate the amount of time change and adoption takes. Think about it: when your Wi-Fi does not connect within a matter of seconds, if it takes a full minute to connect, it feels like too long – a minute! Many of us also use delivery services that allow us to receive goods within a day or a couple of hours, because waiting the typical three to five days is now considered too long.

When it comes to change and adoption, we tend to apply those same principles or ethos, and this is when, as leaders, we really do ourselves a disservice. If we think about death or birth, the amount of time it takes us to adjust to news of either can be a matter of days or even months (and sometimes years). That is because death and birth are typically big changes, which take time to accept – the same amount of time needs to be allowed for significant organizational change. We need to recognize that when we are fundamentally changing the way people work, which is what real organizational transitioning is; it will take months and quite possibly years to adopt. And we also need to remember that the higher the level of resistance, the more time will be required.

As leaders, we need to recognize this and factor time into any and all plans, and do our utmost to try and minimize the level of resistance. We need to be clear and upfront with ourselves, as well as the rest of the organization, about the length of time required to achieve the ultimate goal of change, whether that is two years or five years. The upside is, if change happens sooner, which could be the case, then you have a brilliant good news story you can really market and shout out about. If it happens within the time indicated, then again you have a good news story you can market and shout out about. It is only if it takes longer than you stated that you don't feel you quite have the good news story you hoped. Take the example of the Crossrail railway construction project in the UK. Crossrail said for years (and stated in several news stories and television programmes) that progress was going well and that the project would definitely be delivered on time in 2018. Then, a few months before it was supposed to be launched, Crossrail announced that it was not going to complete the project within the expected timeframe. This had a big impact on the reputation of individuals and organizations involved. So do yourself a favour and factor in a realistic amount of time for the change to take place, and then add on at least another six months to a year to be safe.

DEFINING THE FIRST STEP IN THE ABCHANGE MODEL

Once you have answered the organizational development questions in the previous section, you should be able to identify the type of change you are leading or managing. In the ABChange model, there are six types of change, based on Goleman's theories (2002). When determining which type of change most suits your situation, it is best to think about the root cause or catalyst for the change, based on the answers to the questions above. For example, many people think if they are planning a fundamental change to their organization, that means it is radical. However, in actuality it might not be radical, but rather it is about improving how the organization operates so they can differentiate themselves further from their competitors.

Take a look at the list below and really ask yourself – what is the ultimate purpose of this change? Once you have identified it, challenge yourself – is this really why we are doing it – the ultimate goal? Is there no other root cause? And if there is, then what is the most important reason or purpose for this change – what makes it so critical it happens?

1. **Bring about radical change:** when you are aiming to make a fundamental change to the operations of an organization.
2. **Make an improvement:** when the core reason for the organization to make the change is to improve either people, processes, systems or performance.
3. **Heal discourse:** when there may have been a good deal of upheaval or conflict within the organization (perhaps for some time), and a change needs to happen to address and heal the discourse.
4. **Build buy-in and consensus:** when the purpose of the change is to have a number of people involved and completely bought into the change, in order to get it down. Their consensus to make it happen is critical reason to make the change happen. This is a change that I think is many times overlooked. Lots of people say to me, well of course we need buy in – we need people to collaborate, but I would ask, is this at the core of the change? Is this why it needs to happen?
5. **Get high performance from an already motivated team:** when you are leading a change when the team is highly motivated and you need to get a high performance from them. For example, if you have a team of graduates that have just come on board (and so are excited about being at the company and at work, etc.) and you need to get them to perform at a high level, this may require some fundamental changes for them because they have not worked in a professional environment before.

6. **Deal with a crisis or emergency:** this is rarely planned and luckily does not happen very often. This type of change is self-explanatory, in the sense if there is a crisis or emergency at its core. An example of this might be when the global pandemic happened, and there was a sudden requirement for people to wear masks, shop, work and travel very differently.

Once you have identified the type of change, the ABChange model outlines the rest for you. However, if the wrong type of change is identified, then unfortunately you will not implement the change effectively, greatly increasing the risk of it not being a success. For example, the World Health Organization wanted to implement a surgical safety checklist, which proved to save lives in the operating theatre when followed. It could be argued (and has been confidentially confirmed) that this change was rolled out as a radical change for the medical profession and a visionary leadership style was used. In fact, this was actually a change that needed buy-in and consensus, requiring a democratic leadership style. Due to this error, the change did not occur at the level required or recommended, and today there are many operating theatres around the world that are not utilizing the safety checklist (Treadwell, Lucas and Tsou 2014).

KEY POINTS

- Sponsorship is the number one success factor for change.

- It is important to identify the best person to sponsor the change:
    1. someone with influence on senior executives, who will be active and visible
    2. someone who can give permission for resources to be used and supported for the change to happen.

- Leaders need to build enthusiasm for the change throughout the whole network: with the executive sponsor, managers, champions, project team and key stakeholders.

- It is vital to communication the 'why' of change in a way that will ensure others listen.

- An organizational development approach is needed to identify the right type of change through challenging questions.

- Factoring in enough time is critical to successful change management. Leaders should be realistic about how long the change will take, and then add more to the timeline.

REFLECTIVE QUESTIONS

- What is the ultimate purpose or root cause for your change?

- What will the impact be of too much or too little time before the change happens?

CHAPTER 3

The ABChange Model

THE MODEL EXPLAINED

The foundations of change (Burnes 2004), types of change (Dunphy and Stace 1993) and steps of change (Mitchell and Larson 1989) are all related, as they all try to define change. For example, the foundations of change define where change may come from, the types of change define what kind of change may be occurring, and the steps of change define how the change happens.

Figure 3: The ABChange model

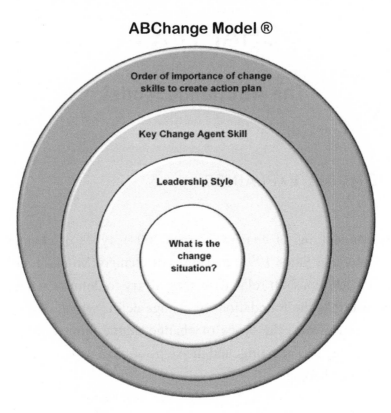

Source: Bryan 2009.

However, they do not tell us how we are to lead and or manage change. According to Goleman, 'research has shown that the most successful leaders have strengths in self- awareness, self-regulation, motivation, empathy and social skill' (Goleman 2000, p. 77), implying working relationships are key to being a successful leader and I would argue in leading and influencing change. A major mistake managers could make is to assume leadership is only a function of personality rather than a strategic choice.

The aim of the research, when creating the ABChange model (see Figure 3), was to examine how leadership skills impact organizational change. The objectives were to examine the models of leadership; explore the potential link between leadership behaviour and organizational change; review change agent skills of those who look to promote/support/sponsor or help deliver and implement change (Kanter 1989), and how these skills are linked to change situations; and identify a potential link between leadership styles and different change situations.

During the analysis of the research conducted, it was concluded that the leadership styles and situations, based on Goleman (2002), directly correlated with specific change skills, based on Kanter (1989). This set out the priorities and created a practical model for managers to easily follow and use in leading change.

So, if you have answered all the questions in the previous chapter, then you should have a good idea as to the type of change you are dealing with, managing or leading. This is the first step in the ABChange model. It is also the most critical step, as stated before, because if you define the wrong change, then you may embark on a path that is not suitable for your change, and hence it could go very, very wrong. I would strongly encourage you make sure you have the most complete answers to those questions and to be realistic with yourself as to what the vision and goals and ultimate purpose of the change (by the way, don't forget about the timescales).

Once the leader or manager has identified the type of change with which they are dealing, then the ABChange model defines what they need to do to lead people through the change: what leadership style they need to exhibit, and the change skills in order of priority (see Table 1). This is not to say that some of the actions of the change skills should or could not happen in tandem. It is the order of priority of the skills, not actions, which is key, and hence if you spend more time on the lowest ranked skill rather than the highest ranked skill, then I can guarantee the change is not going to be managed effectively (Bryan 2009).

Table 1. Leaderships styles and skills required for different types of change

Type of Change Situation	Leadership Style	Most important skill	Other skills ranked in importance
Radical Change	Visionary	Build Trust	Collaborate, work across business functions, stake reward, self confidence, respect change process, work independently
Improvement	Coaching	Build Trust	Collaborate, self confidence, work across business units, stake reward, respect change process, work independently
Healing Discourse	Affiliative	Trust, Self Confidence and Collaborate	Work independently, stake reward, work across business units, respect change process
Build buy-in, consensus	Democratic	Trust and Collaborate	Self confidence, work across business units, respect change process, work independently, stake reward
Get high performance from motivated team	Pace-Setting	Self Confidence	Build trust, work across business units, collaborate, stake reward, respect change process, work independently
Crisis, emergency	Commanding	Self Confidence	Work independently, collaborate, stake reward, build trust, work across business function, respect change process.

Source: Bryan 2009.

During the analysis of my research, it was noted that many managers were aware they typically preferred a particular leadership style, but that they did not always understand why that style would not be appropriate for certain situations. Even though they recognized they did not necessarily adapt their style, they were aware of the positive or negative impact this had on their team members.

This is a pitfall, I have noticed, that many managers or leaders fall into; when leading change, you need to utilize the right style of leadership for the right situation. This means that you need to interpret the style of leadership personally and draw out what that style means to you. For example, how I define myself being democratic and how you may define yourself may be slightly different. So we need to really ask ourselves what this means and as a result, what difference could this make in leading our change? We also need to ask this same question for the change skills. If the most important change skill is self-confidence, then how do I demonstrate that? Really drawing this out will help us develop our change plans and will also make it all more personal and start to answer the big question commonly asked, 'What do I do with this change sitting on my desk?'

Furthermore, as shown in Table 1, if a manager or leader is implementing a healing discourse type of change, then the leadership style they will need to demonstrate is affiliative. There are then three primary skills the manager will need to focus on: building trust, having self-confidence and collaboration. The key is for the manager to define specifically how they will ensure they use an affiliative leadership style, along with how they will implement the three skills and what impact that will have on the change (i.e., building trust takes time – how does that fit into the timeline for change? Who do they need to build trust with and how will they know they have accomplished their goal?).

HOW MANAGERS HAVE USED THE MODEL

Due to my previous work experience with a financial services client, I was asked by a new supplier to come in and help on a particular project. This project was in quite a state – the individual previously responsible had been signed off sick by their doctor due to the stress of the situation, and when I listened in on the first project meeting... oh my goodness, the amount of hostility, distrust and blame going on was at epidemic levels. As a result, the entire project was at risk of not being completed, much less on time. I recognized immediately that the change that needed to happen as a priority was to heal the discourse within the project team.

I immediately started to implement my definition of an affiliative leadership style for this situation. This included prioritizing the individuals within the project team that I needed to start building a relationship with (the client first) and asking, as the new person, if I could meet with them individually later on in the week. I then asked them about their concerns, issues, challenges, frustrations and what they ultimately wanted – including their vision, objectives and change requirements. I just sat and took notes, empathized and sympathized with their feelings. I also promised them I would be talking to everyone and would share some actions with them by the following week, first individually, then as a group in the next project team meeting after the actions were agreed. Then I would hold everyone accountable to those agreements, publicly, so it was clear what needed to happen, how and by when.

This enabled me to demonstrate the prioritized skills of building trust and collaboration, but it also took a good deal of self-confidence to call people out if they did not stick to what had been agreed, which did happen the first couple of weeks. Once that was achieved though, the team started to operate in a much more cohesive way and the project was put back on track, and as a result was delivered on time.

Another example is Alice, who had been leading a team, as its manager, for three years before a very radical business change meant that a majority of her staff would lose their jobs. Working with her coach, Alice had to call upon her past experiences with team members to build their trust in this change. She shared as much information as she possibly could with them and gave them specific deadlines as to when she would have answers to their questions. If she missed the deadline, she told them when she would be able to get back to them and why she did not have the information when she had originally promised. This enabled Alice to continue building the trust she had with her team through this very radical and difficult change.

A further example is an agency within central government that had the goal of transforming its customer service network. This entailed the closure of 39 offices across the UK; redeployment or redundancy of 170 employees; relocation of 100 employees to nearby offices; re-grading of 270 employees to a lower grade; introduction of new roles; introduction of remotely managed 'flexible teams'; and centralization of services.

Each of the areas above were being run as separate projects within a change programme, all of which were due to be complete within 18 months of the initial announcement. This change was also happening at the same time as a series of organizational restructures; some of these changes were part of the overarching programme and others were being delivered independently.

There were a number of key issues with this change programme and how it was being led and managed:

• The biggest issue faced by the change programme was an announcement of the change was made to the organization without a plan or strategy for how to implement the actions required. This was the first large-scale downsizing the organization had ever implemented. There was no precedent for how it should be led and managed and the staff were very shocked – redundancies had not been part of the working culture. This meant the staff felt the psychological contract had been broken.
• There were extremely high levels of resistance at all levels, including throughout management in and outside the scope.

Effectively, once the big decision had been made that this change was to happen, people buried their heads in the sand hoping it would go away. This delayed decisions being made on any strategy or further planning.

- Middle management did not engage with staff on issues. This meant the only messages staff received were from senior management, which created a vacuum in people management.
- There were further issues with the location of staff, as they were geographically spread across the UK in small offices of six to eight people. Many of these offices were being closed as a result of the change and staff were either being redeployed or made redundant.
- With middle management not engaging with staff, all people saw was redundancy and closure; people became very angry and were left alone with these emotions.
- When middle management did arrive at the office, they were faced with highly charged negative emotions. Hence they started to try and create false realities to appease staff and get out of the firing line.

So, what did the project team do and how? They applied the ABChange model, which helped them reconsider the entire change programme. They started to have conversations about why the change was necessary and how it fit into the future of the organization. The biggest impact the model had for the team was to redefine the change programme by definition and scope from an execution of logistics and resources to managing people through redeployment and redundancy, this being a radical change for the organization. Previously, the change had been defined by the organization as removal of IT and sending out communications, not as being about people. The ABChange model highlighted that change is about people not IT, and that it required a visionary leadership style. The model also helped the team in a number of ways:

- It confirmed the overall scale of the change facing the existing network in becoming the new customer network. It focused discussion on the entirety of the activity rather than individual projects.
- It focused discussion on the lack of a combined and bought into vision for the end state of the transformation.
- It drove discussion about the complexity of communicating an unclear vision and the relationship between projects in and outside the programme.
- It helped focus discussions on the visibility of senior management and the levels of trust in them from the affected employees.
- It enabled discussion on roles and responsibilities for delivering change between line managers and projects.
- It began conversations on how much information and support is required to enable managers to deliver change.
- It focused thinking on the resources required to support employees through this change.

After applying the ABChange model, the team decided there needed to be a vision for the organization, and some consideration of how this significant change would impact that vision. This vision gave people who were still working in the organization a true picture of the place where they worked, thus reassuring them of their own future within the organization. The vision was achieved through a number of actions:

- Formal decisions were made on the design of the end state.
- Communication messages were centralized.
- Project activity was refocused to better support line managers rather than staff.
- The visibility of line managers was increased, rather than project resources.
- The team worked with the Director of Operational Change to plot and align related changes across the organization.

The real added value the team believes the ABChange model gave them was the ability to uncover the root causes of the issues they were facing. The model highlighted the need for the change team to stop managing staff directly. Instead they needed to provide support with strict instructions to managers to manage staff directly. Looking at the leadership styles and how to manage and lead people through this specific change made the team realize they needed to change their style and the way they interacted with staff in leading this organizational change.

WHY THE ABCHANGE MODEL HELPS LEAD CHANGE

Learning requires individuals within an organization to understand the assumptions, frameworks and norms guiding the business activity in order to challenge and change these norms, as and when necessary (Morgan 1997). This implies senior managers need to undergo a degree of learning in order to challenge the status quo and influence change within an organization.

The question driving the research that developed this model was: 'How does behaviour link to leadership styles and change agent skills, and how do these relate to change situations?'

The aim was to examine these relationships and explore how best to influence change. As part of this research and process of linking the two theories, a range of senior managers were interviewed and two questions were asked in relation to the variety of situations where change was required:

* What are your perceptions of what leadership approaches are or are not appropriate for this situation?
* What skills do you think you need to manage this situation?

The research reviewed the perceived skills the managers thought they needed in order to influence change. Each situation was then mapped against Goleman's leadership styles, according to which style the managers through was appropriate or inappropriate.

Kanter's change agent skills could then be ranked order of priority for each of the change situations.

Considering the research was based on the feedback of participants, reflective learning played a crucial role in the research process. Reflective learning for transformation typically occurs when individuals question and challenge assumptions and 'taken-for-granteds' (McGill and Brockbank 2004). This definition was used as the basis of the interview process because the participants were asked to reflect back to their personal experiences to give specific examples and explanations for most of the questions.

The leadership questions and the change-agent skill questions were separated in the actual interviews and therefore the participants could not make direct links between the leadership styles and the change situations. However, in the analysis, the descriptions and reasoning behind the answers to these questions indicates a direct link can be made between these two elements.

When the participants' 360-degree feedback was reviewed, a link was made between their ability to adapt their leadership styles and their ability to influence change. Taking this into account – as well as the links made between Kanter's change skills and Goleman's leadership styles and change situations – the ABChange model was created. Once a manager identifies the type of change situation he or she needs to implement, they can use the ABChange model to identify the leadership style they need to exemplify and the most important skills required to implement this change effectively.

As a result, due to the practicalities of the ABChange model, leaders and managers are able to create actions plans that enable them to effectively manage and implement their specific change, hence improving the outcomes of the change on the organization and their influencing factors.

KEY POINTS

- Identifying the type of change is the first and most critical step of the ABChange model.

- Change skills are not a 'to do' list; many will happen in tandem.

- A manager or leader should define what each type of leadership and change skill means to them; this is how an approach to leadership becomes personal.

REFLECTIVE QUESTIONS

- Take another look at Table 1: what behaviours define each type of leadership style to you?

- How will you know you are adopting that style of leadership? How will others know?

- How will you implement the most important change skill(s)?

- How will this impact the change itself?

CHAPTER 4

The Future of Leadership in ABChange

The definition of leadership according to Roger Bennett is 'the ability to influence the thoughts and behaviour of others' (1997, p. 196). This may explain why the development of leadership skills is typically focused on analysing and changing behaviour.

Through my work, I have found that many managers and leaders want to put people through formulaic change processes and apply standardized definitions of change. The issue is that A plus B does not equal C when it comes to managing people; there is not even a guarantee that you will get the same outcome in the same situation with the same person. This is because the emotional state or situation of the individual (including the manager themselves) will vary at different points in life, and even moment by moment.

Goleman (2002, p. 3) states, 'great leadership works through the emotions... no matter what leaders set out to do – their success depends on how they do it.' He argues that their emotions or actions influence individual performance through leadership, which leads to possible change within that organization. I agree with this statement

– I mean, how can they not? For example, my children, at different points in their lives, have been working towards particular goals and each time they are encouraged with positive reinforcement. They achieve much higher results through this reinforcement than they ever have done with criticism. Even when you think the criticism is constructive, without that positive reinforcement individuals lose motivation and desire – the task becomes a chore, and their brains do not function as well in the situation as they would otherwise.

THE RELATIONSHIP BETWEEN WORKPLACE AND LEADERSHIP

There are a numerous books, theories, practices, blogs and articles (the list goes on…) on different styles of leadership (see Table 2). For example, the trait approach was greatly used during the Industrial Revolution, when the workplace required a great deal more command and control from leadership in order to give people instructions on what and how to do things. In this situation, there was very little room for people to divert from the instructions in order to complete the task at hand (Bryan 2014). Then there are the contingency and situational leadership styles and theories that were developed by Fiedler (1967), Hersey and Blanchard (1969) and Goleman (2000). These theories are still popular today and I would argue are still required to help tailor leadership style to the needs of the people and situation accordingly.

Table 2: The relationship between workplace and leadership style

Date	Workplace	Leadership style	Motivation and engagement
Pre 1900–1920	Factory	Trait approach	Scientific management
1940–1980	Plural and cubicle office	Contingency and situational	Hierarchy of needs
1980–2000	Open plan	Transformational	Psychological contract
2000–2018	Agile workspace	Emotional intelligence	Work/life balance
2018–present	Consumer centric	Holistic	Autonomy

Source: Bryan 2014.

During the period from 1980 to 2000, the transformational leadership style required the charisma of the individual to instigate transformation, in a similar way to the trait leadership style. This helped with the psychological contract that many people felt they entered into when they decided to work for an organization. ('I will work for you, give you my loyalty, time, effort, and you (said company) will give me a salary, security, health insurance', etc.) The issue was when the psychological contract was broken (through redundancy, organization directions changing, re-structuring, etc.). This generated a great deal of cynicism in the workplace, and can still happen in some situations today.

More recently, the age of agile workspaces has created, yet again, a transition towards leadership that centres around interpersonal, conceptual and administrative skills. Emotional intelligence is at the forefront; how leaders perceive, plan, organize and solve problems is key to motivating and engaging employees to create a work/life balance.

A leader in a financial institution recently stated, 'The most important skill is obtaining an understanding of the different qualities that people possess and how you need to react differently for people with different styles and adapt accordingly.'

Since 2018, there has been a transition towards a holistic style of leadership. This was driven by a number of changes:

- An increase in self-employment.
- An increase in working from home.
- An increase in a desire for autonomy, creativity and mastery.

These factors take away the need for the psychological contract and replace it with a more transactional relationship: 'I will do this for this amount and no one expects anything else in return, except a job well done.'

According to Hilary Jeffery at AECOM and the research her team conducted a few years ago, the workplace will shift 'from being the centre of productivity to being a core resource and corporate community centre' (Gillen and Jeffery 2014, p. 15). Boundaries have already been further blurred between work and the rest of our lives due to new technology, pace of change and our interaction with the workspace. The workspace will become a consumer environment in which workers and managers alike come to meet colleagues and friends, eat, relax, as well as work alone – much like a city; I believe this approach will only grow over time. It won't be long, in my opinion, until no one will 'go to the office' unless they very specifically need to either meet with someone face to face or use a specific technology that they are unable to purchase or use easily at home – in other words, when they can get 'more' from the office than from working remotely.

Traditionally, the desk was created in the workplace for the use of pen and paper. Then eventually the typewriter was added, then the phone and currently a screen, keyboard, mouse and quite possibly a docking station. I postulate that the need for any and all of these tools are rapidly disappearing. Perhaps they will soon be replaced by voice control and/or an augmented reality (AR) or AR-like visor that is no more cumbersome to the staff member than a headset, and all the computing, connecting, collaborating, sharing and creating will be done with and through that 'visor' with the use of AI. The office will become a place where staff only go if they have a requirement to meet face to face: to connect, train or network. The rest of the time, they could meet virtually; homeworking will increase; and more and more spaces will be created as 'coffee shops' for people to conduct their business. Prior to the coronavirus pandemic there was already evidence of this with the creation of WeWork and other similar businesses. Through the pandemic, it has been proven that many people could work from home, when previously this was not an accepted ideology for several roles. Now, going forward, companies are starting to question the amount of office space they need and to what purpose. A hybrid way of working is becoming the accepted 'new' norm, with many people working the majority of their time remotely and coming into the office for specific reasons. As a result of all this, companies will start to create collaborative virtual and real spaces that rebuilds the 'office environment', whilst maintaining the branding and sense of belonging for staff.

So, if that is the type of environment that we could potentially be operating in professionally, what does that mean for leadership and leading through change?

A HOLISTIC APPROACH TO LEADERSHIP

As stated above, the leadership skills of tomorrow will need to match the workplace of the future (much as they have done in the past). Instead of just using emotional intelligence, transitional or situational skills to lead and manage people, a holistic or whole approach and skillset may be required. While the organizational development approach enables a perspective on the whole company, similarly a holistic and planned approach is used to practically manage the organization. It incorporates different elements such as the task, structure, people and technology or environment, with the aim of generating improvement.

For example, the holistic leadership approach could enable a shift to being employee-focused, empowering staff to make decisions and have control over what they do. It incorporates the different elements of a person in work such as task, family, social elements and environment as a way of leading people to generate improvement in a person's life through work-related activities. For example, during lockdown, managers and team members have had to either 'get used' to children or cats or dogs interrupting meetings or schedule around peak 'home life' times to accommodate and combine individual and work needs.

Then the question becomes: how does a leader apply this? First of all, trust needs to be established. The Chartered Institute of Professional Development (CIPD) conducted some research in 2012 that outlined the requirements to build trust, which they called the Pillars of Trust (Dietz and Den Hartog 2006):

- Ability to be perceived as leading
- Benevolence to others
- Integrity
- Predictability.

What do these mean with regard to the types of behaviours a leader will need in the environment of the future? Being perceived as having an ability to do something means there is a degree of confidence demonstrated. There is also a degree of capability and technical understanding. In leadership terms, this can be demonstrated through emotional intelligence which links directly to being able to demonstrate a level of care and concern for staff.

That means there are already a number of behaviours identified that will be a requirement of leaders going forward: confidence, emotional intelligence, analytical, evaluation and communication. To support these leadership behaviours and define them in the social context of the organization, a set of values is needed. These values create a culture and identity for the organization, which the leaders will need to foster. For example, during the London 2012 Olympics, it was mentioned several times in the media that the strength of London was its diversity. In an organizational context, it could be assumed that the value of the city is diversity, which defines the city's culture and identity. As a result, leaders of the city are encouraged to articulate how diversity is alive and real in the city with visitors and citizens alike. An example of this might be the implementation of the Equalities Act 2010, which several laws and constructs within the city are dictated to follow, such as building disability access in new and renovated train stations. The same type of method also applies to organizations in the sense that and it will be the leaders that will need to encourage, promote and monitor how the organizational values are manifested with the people in their teams.

Morice Mendoza reported that at Netflix the behaviours embedded within the culture of the organization generate a level of performance to get things done. Performance management is about engaging leaders and staff in conversations as an 'organic part of their work' (Mendoza 2014, p. 24). This is very much in line with taking a holistic approach to leadership and management. So, there are a range of skills that will be required for leaders and managers going forward:

- Influencing skills
- Emotional intelligence
- Confidence
- Analytical skills
- Communication
- Technical competence
- Benevolence to others

- Integrity
- Consistency in approach
- Flexibility
- Adaptability.

Therefore, it is reasonable to say that leadership going forward will be about taking a holistic approach to management that incorporates a whole-person approach to staff and teams to help meet the needs of the business. Leaders will need to be able to redefine and ensure boundaries and rules are established through a social context. They will need to have a high level of emotional intelligence to demonstrate benevolence to others and the intellectual capability to get the job done. They will also need an ability to communicate messages consistently and frequently, so staff have a complete awareness of the expectations and requirements of them as a member of the organization in a consumer-like construct.

There are already examples of this approach to leadership in articles published by the *Harvard Business Review*, among other publications. When I was working for an infrastructure company, benevolence to others and taking a much more holistic approach to leadership really came to the fore. To help out with some very key activities, I hired a graduate, who was absolutely amazing and a real go-getter. During one of our settling-in discussions, I mentioned that many people work from home on Fridays, including myself, so if that was something she wanted to do, or if there was another day or two that she would prefer to work from home, that was not an issue; she just needed to let me know, particularly for health and safety reasons. The first Friday, she did come in, but realized the office was quite empty, so the next few weeks she worked from home. About a month went by, and I discovered she was back in the office on a Friday. I thought that was odd, so I asked her why she had gone in. She replied that because she lived in a house share, the only place she could work was in her bedroom, and that was not really a desirable environment for her.

I have to admit, I did not even consider this possibility before-hand, as I very much enjoy working from home; I feel it gives me more of a work/life balance – but then, I live in a house and have a dedicated 'office space', making my circumstances very different. I knew that soon after her graduation she had moved to East Croydon and the organization had an office there. I said to her, if she would prefer go to the office, then why didn't she go to the East Croydon office rather than the central London office, making her commute a fifteen-minute walk rather than a one-hour train ride. She very much appreciated this alternative and continued to work in this way going forward. As a leader, and her manager, I needed to take a holistic approach to dealing with the situation and understand her whole needs, including her personal and professional requirements.

HOLISTIC LEADERSHIP AND THE ABCHANGE MODEL

So, how do we use the holistic leadership approach in change and how does this impact the use of the ABChange model? Essentially, I think the holistic approach is already incorporated into the model because there is the use of the holistic organizational perspective in the steps that help define the type of change.

For example, using the case study shared in the previous chapter of creating a new customer service network, the type of change identified (rather unusually) was radical for the organization and, as discussed, required a completely new vision and approach. Utilizing the visionary leadership style with the holistic leadership approach would mean taking people's individual circumstances into play along with the organization's needs as a whole – which is actually what happened and needed to happen. Leaders and managers needed to take an active role in the change and apply it across the board to enable their teams to adapt to the change, in whatever way required. Furthermore, a leader needs to understand the potential personal support mechanisms or hindrances for the individuals in their team. Remember the example of the graduate I gave earlier – I needed to take into account her personal circumstances of living in a house share and not having a desirable space to work from home and help her come up with an alternative that would meet her needs, while also not feeling isolated in an empty office.

Taking a people approach to change, by using the ABChange model, demonstrates a holistic leadership approach. This is because – regardless of the situation – there will always be a number of changes within any one organizational transformation and therefore a number of leadership styles required during each of those different changes (see Figure 4). However, the overarching leadership approach to deliver change for and with the people is holistic – the whole person and the whole organization is required to help define the right change and lead or manage people in the right and most successful way.

Figure 4: A people approach to change

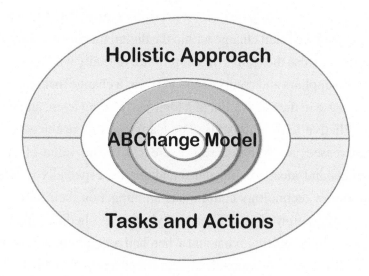

Referring back again to the example of creating a completely new operating model for an infrastructure company – this change, big as it was, was only one small change that was incorporated into a much bigger change – the digital transformation. An overarching holistic leadership approach was required to lead and manage this change, but for each of the changes that sat within the umbrella of that digital transformation a number of different leadership styles were required. The new operating model was very much about building buy-in and consensus across a number of different teams, which required (as per the model) a democratic leadership style because all the different systems and processes were 'owned' by different areas of the business. Each area needed to be involved to some degree and all needed to buy into the reason, purpose and design of the model, in order for it to be implemented and adopted.

Yet another small change within the digital transformation was the need to raise the team's digital profile externally with potential clients, suppliers and competitors. This was a change that required an increase in the motivation of a high-performing team, and thus an affiliative leadership style. The team's confidence needed to be increased, as well as a self-awareness of the value of their thoughts and ideas to colleagues and clients, especially in relation to how technology could make an impact on their industry. The combination of an affiliative style and a scheduled plan of who would be writing what and when had a great impact on the team. It resulted in valuable thought leadership that increased their digital profile externally.

To summarize, a holistic leadership approach refers to the overarching approach to change. The ABChange model can then be applied with the right leadership styles and change skills, followed by the tasks and actions required to enable the adoption of the change to follow.

KEY POINTS

- There is no guarantee that you will get the same results with different people and situations because, when working with people, A plus B does not equal C.

- A holistic leadership approach is required when delivering change. This means taking into account all the different aspects of a person, both within and outside of work (for example, the task itself, family, social factors and environment or space), as a way of leading people to through change.

- Building and having trust is critical in leading change.

- Leaders need to have a high level of emotional intelligence to demonstrate benevolence to others, the intellectual capability to get the job done, and communicate messages consistently and frequently so staff have a complete awareness of the expectations and requirements needed to interact and be a member of the organization in a consumer-like construct.

- Leaders need to know and understand the potential support mechanisms and hindrances for individuals in their teams with change.

- The whole person and whole organization is required to help define the right change and lead people in the right way for successful change.

REFLECTIVE QUESTIONS

- What is the real purpose of this change and how will it impact the individuals on my team?

- What type of support will the individuals in your team need to help them through the change?

CHAPTER 5

Dealing with Resistance

Many leaders I talk to about change seem to really fear the resistance to change among their teams. I would like to reassure you that resistance is natural – we all do it and we should expect it, even with a positive change. For example, if I was to say to you, 'You have just won the lottery and now have £5 million,' your first reaction, naturally, would be to disbelieve it and say, 'No... no, not really. You are pulling my leg... really? Oh my goodness... really?', and so on. Our first reaction to *any* change, even winning the lottery, is to question, disbelieve and, as a result, resist. The Kübler-Ross model (1969) defines the different emotional stages we all go through when confronted with a change. The only variation is time – how long does it take us to go through the emotions or change curve?

REASONS FOR RESISTANCE

So you don't need to worry about resistance – you need to expect it! And to be fair, this is when it all starts to get exciting. Within the change curve, there are those who will go through the change fairly quickly, those who will take a bit longer and those who simply won't change at all and eventually leave. According to Rogers (1962), the innovators and early adopters make up approximately sixteen per cent and the laggards equate to roughly another sixteen per cent. Then there are the early and late majority, which make up approximately sixty-eight per cent, and that is who we need to focus our effort on and where we really need apply our holistic leadership style and use the ABChange model.

In the past chapter, we discussed the role of the holistic leadership approach with the other leadership styles required for the specific change being managed and lead. Taking all that into consideration, when it comes to dealing with resistance there needs to be a recognition that the whole person, and not just part of the person, will need to be managed and lead. You may wonder why I would say such a thing, as of course we are managing a whole person. However, I would argue that many times we expect to only manage the 'professional' person. And we all know that we are not always 'professional' – we have personal lives too, and with the whole person comes emotions. We need to get comfortable and resolute in the fact that we need to help others (and ourselves) manage, lead and deal with emotions.

I don't mean our 'manage' in the sense of hiding our emotions – exactly the opposite. We need to be able to share our emotions, but when it comes to managing and leading, we need to be able to do this in a controlled and constructive way, which can be difficult. Sharing our own emotions can be very powerful, because it shows people we are human and we feel – how many times have you thought your manager must be stone cold or superhuman to not react? However, we need to be able to show our emotions without losing control, as that is less powerful.

Likewise, we also need to learn how to cope when someone else is emotional. What will we do when someone cries? Will we pretend it is not happening, which typically happens now? I would suggest reacting in the same way we would do with a friend – get them a tissue, pull them aside and ask what is wrong and/or whether you can help in any way. Another challenging emotion is when someone shouts: will we run away and hide? Bury our head? Or face it head on? When someone is shouting, they are usually expressing some anger or frustration. So how would we deal with a friend like this – again pull them aside and ask if they need to take a walk or get some air and then offer to talk about it when they get back.

How we deal with emotion in our personal lives now will transpire into the workplace, as both places meld into one. Expecting the behaviour of 'professional' will need to actually disappear as no one person will always be professional. I am not saying we treat all the people in work as our friends but, during emotional moments, it is that level of empathy that is needed from leaders.

We also need to notice what people are not saying by reading tone, body language and changes in verbal or written communication. For example, if someone sends an email using very different language from the one they have used in the past, we as managers need to notice and take note – chances are the individual is trying to express a strong emotion that we then need to manage or help them with.

Now not everyone will react emotionally and not at the same time or in the same way. This will mean during change that sometimes people will be emotionally in sync with one another, sometimes they will complement each other and sometimes they will be doing their own thing – which can be and feel lonely. We will need to be aware of this and again try to manage it. Whatever the case may be, we will need to accept, adapt and cope with this emotional boundary.

So we have talked about emotions that we all go through with change, but what about resistance? Is all resistance emotional? The simple answer to this is no – there are six other reasons why people resist, from my experience:

- Self-interest
- Psychological factors
- Change approach
- Recipient perceptions
- Cultural bias
- Historic organizational reasons
- Emotional factors.

CHAPTER 5

TACTICS FOR MANAGING RESISTANCE

SELF-INTEREST

When someone is resisting due to self-interest, it is because they perceive the change will have a negative impact on them in some way, such as a change in their status. A good way of managing this type of resistance is to make the individual a champion of the change. This will enable them not only to know a great deal about the change (and hence have a good understanding of the change), it will also elevate their status (which they possibly perceived to decrease otherwise), because they will need to collaborate and communicate with multiple people in order to be a real champion or agent of the change.

PSYCHOLOGICAL FACTORS

Psychological reasons for resistance are often related to the fear of change or stress. Many times, this is only a perception, and through coaching, a leader or manager can help an individual with this type of resistance. This can be time-consuming depending on the level of fear, so that may need to be taken into consideration. Is this person critical to the team or work going forward? Would it be a major shame to lose them? If so, then the investment is valuable. If not, then you may want to consider limiting the level of investment.

Furthermore, it is very important when dealing with this type of resistance to understand the level of fear. By that I mean: is the fear so extreme that is a phobia? This may sound like a step too far, but I have worked with a number of organizations where some people have a real phobia of technology and will do whatever they can to avoid it, whenever possible. If this is the case, then the amount and level of coaching will also need to be greater to help the individual get through their phobia, and it may require additional external support as well.

CHANGE APPROACH

Many times, how the change is initially communicated or managed can create a level of resistance. Let's go back to the case study I shared with you earlier regarding creating a new customer service network. Unfortunately the people impacted by this change initially found out through a news report on the radio rather than through their managers and leaders, and this had a damaging impact, as you could imagine, that raised the level of resistance considerably. This is why it is critical that all change, whenever remotely possible, should be planned and managed with the people in mind first and foremost. This can easily be done by involving people as much as possible – consult with them, identify focus groups and get their feedback. This goes beyond just running pilots or having test groups. This is about creating one or several small groups of people; sharing with them the change (direction, vision, objectives, purpose, why, etc.), and asking for their opinions on the change itself. You can also ask how they think their colleagues will respond and what they think would be the best way for people to receive information and become aware of the change, so desire for the change is developed and they can make positive decisions. You can then use this information to create the change and communication plan. This will typically enable the change to have a more positive impact when it is launched more widely.

RECIPIENT PERCEPTIONS

This reason for resistance is based on a lack of understanding or awareness of the change and many times is due to a miscommunication of some sort. So the best way to manage this resistance is to use multiple communication styles. For example, start out using a coaching style to really understand their perception and then demonstrate how their perception is different from the actual change. You could also ask them what it is about the change that concerns them the most, and then show them how the change is different or perhaps similar to what they are fearing, and reassure them that you will do your best to alleviate those concerns.

It is critical to empathize and sympathize with the individuals who are resistant. Showing your concern and emotions helps demonstrate you are listening and are here to help, as and when you can, to lead them through the change.

CULTURAL BIAS

This is typically expressed by someone saying, 'We don't do that around here.' This is a more common reason for resistance than many managers or leaders realize, whenever a change is regarding a fundamental way in which people work, whether that be a change to the environment of the workspace or technology, or a completely new policy or process that will fundamentally change their 'everyday'. A way of managing this type of resistance is to really listen to the reasons why the change is not applicable to the culture of the organization. What is it regarding the norms of the working day that will make this change challenging? Then ask your team what they think needs to happen in order for the change to actually work. This way you are able to really understand their perspective, deal with any concerns and even potentially create a win/win situation by committing to further actions, not previously considered, in order to 'fix' the cultural challenge.

HISTORIC ORGANIZATIONAL REASONS

Out of all the reasons to resist, this one can be really quite tricky, because it stems from the understanding that the organization tried the change before and it did not work. So, it is critical to know this from the outset – don't hide from it. In fact, you should highlight what the change was last time, recognize the issues and why it failed. Then you will need to be very clear in how this change is different. You should think about how previous challenges are being considered or dealt with and managed; how the change is different from the previous time; why it is important that the change succeeds this time; what you and the whole organization need to make it happen (whether this is greater financial investment, more people involved, processes or policies change to help, etc.).

With all of these different reasons to resist, it is critical to really take into account the whole person, as discussed earlier – listen, and I mean really listen: hear what they are saying, how they are saying it and what they are not saying in the way they are saying it.

Does it sound like a lot and is it complicated for us as a leader to manage? – yes. Is it a lot and complicated for us? – yes. It's people, not rocket science. We are humans, not robots, so no algorithm or formula can 'fix' the issues and put everything right. We need to understand that we all have emotions, we will all go through them at different rates and we will all have our own moments of resistance, even when we are positive about a change. We need to accept that is OK – genuinely OK. It does not mean we have failed, or that we are terrible, or that it is all crap – it just means we are human and we are working with other humans, and as a result, we will resist, one way or another. And that is fine – we just need to spot the signs and manage the resistance using the different tactics outlined in this chapter, based on the different reasons for resistance.

KEY POINTS

- Resistance is natural and should be expected.

- Get comfortable and resolute in the fact that we need to help people (and ourselves) manage, lead and deal with emotions.

- Sharing our own emotions, constructively, can be very powerful.

- During emotional moments, we as leaders need to use a level of empathy we would have for a friend, expressing that same emotion to our team.

- There seven different ways in which people resist change. We, as leaders, need to spot the signs – verbal and non-verbal – that indicate the root cause of the resistance, so we can mitigate the resistance levels and manage it.

- Listen! Really listen – to what they are saying, how they are saying, and what they are not saying and how they are not saying it.

REFLECTIVE QUESTIONS

- What have I heard and seen from my team members when they have gone through change before – either in the business or in their personal lives?

- How will I make sure I am really listening to my team?

CHAPTER 6

How Culture Impacts Change

As we have already stated, change is happening all around us at an exponential rate – this is not news; all we have to do is open our eyes. Technological developments are impacting how we consume content through television (notice I did not say 'watch a television show'), how adverts target their audience, how we read the news, and in how we communicate with each other personally and professionally. Technology is enabling these changes faster than we can really comprehend in many ways, but what does this say about our culture? We still don't have a complete understanding of the impact of big data, smart city initiatives and General Data Protection Regulation (GDPR), but the evidence is there, and nowhere more starkly than in the congressional sessions carried out with Mark Zuckerberg of Facebook in 2018.

Organizations also need to consider possible impacts when they are embarking on a change – the culture of the organization needs to be taken into consideration, as this can determine how ready the organization is for the change. Furthermore, if the culture is not considered then the change could be completely undermined and as a result, fail.

So what do we do? How do we determine and take into consideration the culture of an organization? What do we need to do to ensure the culture adjusts to the change we are trying to implement?

EFFECTIVE STAKEHOLDER ENGAGEMENT

The key to a culture change is stakeholder engagement and management. It is not enough to simply communicate (or, as I say, 'download information') to the key stakeholders. This is about taking them on the journey – enabling them to be your champion, critical friend and sponsor of the change. The key difference is to share with them not only what you are trying to achieve and why, but also get their input. What do they think about it? How do they think this will impact their business areas and teams? What can you do to help them? Do some compromises need to be made as a consequence?

Once you have your key stakeholders on board, it is then about keeping them on board and in the loop. Provide regular updates in the way they would like to receive them, whether that is through a fortnightly, monthly or quarterly meeting, newsletter or email. Whichever way, it is important to make sure they have heard the messages and hence are part of the change itself. You should then look at how you can help everyone else come on board. Is that via a town-hall meeting or workshop, or by utilizing change champions to help spread the word? There are a number of tactics, and the best methods will be determined by the size and location of the organization, along with the number of people who need to receive information. For example, a small organization of 300 may all work predominately in one location, so a town-hall meeting might be best, along with a showcase and drop-in centres. In comparison, a large organization spread across the globe might need champions, local leader sponsorship and use of electronic channels, such as videos, virtual chats and question-and-answer sessions.

The key to integrating real change is to embed the change into how an organization does things – in the processes, procedures and interactions. When it comes to organizational change, typically the process and procedures are thoroughly considered, but interactions are rarely dealt with. Interactions include the behaviours, communication mechanisms and socialization of people with the organization.

When implementing change, you need to consider not just how you want people to interact in the future, but how different that is to the way things are done currently and in what ways this will differ. Then you need to work with the people affected and ask them what they need to do differently and how, or rather what and how they could do things differently. This is a very powerful way of not only giving ownership of the change to the people affected, but also of implementing culture change. After all, it is the people that change a culture – whether that is in an organization, city or society – not a piece of paper.

Brand has a large impact on culture. It includes the values and vision of an organization, as well as how these are manifested. When we look at how to brand a change, often there is a vision for the change, but many times it is a bit wholly and there isn't a clear message or image of how that translates to reality. This is really important, as creating an image enables people to visualize the future and what it means to them. When we can see the direction we are going, we are more likely to actually get there. We also need to ensure this vision of change is hooked into the broader organizational vision, as this helps illustrate the why and relationship of the change to the overarching organization's vision.

The image then needs to be used across all the communications about the change, with a reiteration of how this change is enabling the organizational vision. This reinforces not only the need for the change, but reminds people of the behaviour changes that correlate with the change, thus increasing the adoption rate of the change.

USING ABCHANGE IN REMOTE WORKING

Earlier we talked about the organizational development approach to identifying the type of change we are looking to lead and manage. We have also talked about the different types of communications and understanding how people within our organization send and receive key messages. As we progress to a more remote working environment, which I would argue is the direction of travel for most organizations and their people, we need to really take a look at the direct and indirect messages we send about change and about the organization. For example, there have been a number of studies on how email can be damaging to effective communication, simply because so many of us receive numerous emails a day and struggle to keep up with our inboxes, ending up with hundreds of unread emails. Prosci (2018) has done further studies on this, looking at which communications we are more likely to open and read (these tend to be messages from those we work more closely with – our team members and direct managers). So if this is the case, and we are working more remotely, then what do we do?

Some research has been conducted by Advanced Workplace Associates and Amsterdam-based Centre for Evidence-Based Management (CEBMa) on the elements in the workplace that are needed for optimum performance, and this includes remote working environments. These are called the six factors (Barends, Briner, Mawson, Plum, Rousseau 2014) – social cohesion, perceived supervisory support, information sharing, vision and goal clarity and external communication and trust. However the three that really affect remote working are trust, social cohesion and information sharing, which supports what we have been talking about throughout this book (Mawson 2020). When delivering change particularly, leaders need to focus a good deal of their attention on these three areas because, as we know, it is people who will enable the change to happen.

Building trust, which is one of the most important change skills for a number of the different types of change (see Table 1), is critical and takes time, so that needs to be factored into the change plans, as previously discussed. There also needs to be an understanding of who leaders need to build that trust with, as it will not only be in their direct teams but also with teams that are not under their direction, thus creating the need for social cohesion throughout these areas, along with active and visible sponsorship and leadership. Sharing information helps us achieve change, both by ensuring people are aware of the what, when where, why and how (along with the other areas we have already discussed), but also by building trust. This helps to create the culture needed to lead change successfully.

Technology and space can really enable us to make a change, but we need to make sure we have the right technology and space and use them effectively. For example, we need to recognize the difference between collaboration and communication tools – they are not always the same. Collaboration tools enable people to work collaboratively, which seems obvious, but this does not mean just getting a bunch of people together and talking things out in an audio or video call. Collaboration tools enable the group to be involved, take notes and think collectively. Although a remote verbal or even video call is helpful, other tools are also needed. This would be the same in an open-plan office – if you get a group of people together around a desk, the level of collaboration is hindered by the limits of the space, and this is also disruptive to others nearby. Typically, you would need a meeting room or collaboration space (with flipcharts, a projector, post-its, etc.), to really enable a collaborative activity.

In remote working, as leaders we need to really understand what it is we are trying to achieve, and then look at the tools that will enable us to do that in a virtual and real space. For example, with an activity like a town-hall meeting – traditionally this would be delivered in a large space and people would join in a real environment and, if they could not make it, would receive the slides afterwards and find anything critical out from colleagues. In a more remote-working culture, I would suggest you would need to live-stream the town-hall meeting, and create some virtual activities in the 'marketplace' so colleagues can join in a virtual arena, if they are unable to join in a real environment. This will greatly increase the level of impact and engagement from people across the whole business – suddenly the one town-hall activity can be seen and delivered across all the locations and teams within the business, creating a greater consistency of messages than before.

So we need to be more self-aware and thoughtful about how, when and where we connect, and what technology and space is going to enable the best outcomes. We need to consider what messages we need to get across and how best to really make that happen for all the people we need to impact, taking into account the whole person.

KEY POINTS

- Change is happening, and at an exponential rate.

- The culture of an organization can determine how ready that organization is for change.

- Leaders should take their stakeholders on a journey of change – as a champion, critical friend or sponsor of change.

- Stakeholders should be constantly engaged through regular updates and communications, so they stay part of the change.

- The change should be embedded in how the organization does things – processes, procedures and interaction.

REFLECTIVE QUESTIONS

- What type of positive image will help people visualize the change?

- How can I get the different stakeholders involved so they support the change?

CONCLUSIONS

In this book, we have taken a look at what change management is, how it differs from communication and how communication can help or hinder us in leading and managing change. We have shared multiple examples of how others have implemented change, successfully and otherwise; reviewed the components of the ABChange model and how that can help us lead in change.

We have discussed the importance of asking the right questions before starting a change – taking a holistic approach with leadership and the organization so we can ensure the people and the organization are actually ready for the change. We have also looked at how we need to consider these elements at multiple levels:

1. The organization overall, so the project and sponsorship team can lead the organization through the change.
2. The departments, so the heads can consider all the business impacts the change will have on their teams and the business.
3. The teams, so line managers can understand the potential individual and group impacts of the change.

We need to remember that we will all resist change at some point – we need to not be afraid of resistance or the emotional side of change. Instead, we need to plan for, anticipate, cope with and manage resistance. What is important is that each level of the organization and individual will respond to the change at different times and over different periods of time. As managers or leaders of change, we need to really analyse the impact of the change and view it from the perspective of the group or individuals that are affected.

Good clear, concise and regular communication that is appropriate for the target audience and culture of the organization is also required to help enable the change to happen. Without it, people will not know what they need to do when, much less why they need to do it. Communications need to form a part of the change plan and be designed so the people affected by the change understand and know what is required, not only from the change, but more specifically from themselves, and ensure they have the capability to make it happen. Appropriate planning of change, leadership and communication will greatly determine the level of success and degree of adoption for the 'new business as usual'. A real articulation of how the change will impact different teams and functions across the business, including leadership styles and skills, will help ensure the right strategy, plan and tactics are used at the right time for the specific organization, hence increasing the level of speed and adoption of organizational change.

CONCLUSIONS

Lastly, regardless of all the planning, application and analysis we do, as leaders and managers of change, we need to always remember that things change in the middle, at the start, near the start, near the end, all the time – our plans will not always go to plan. So when that happens, we need to take a step back, reassess the situation, understand the new perspective from the people's point of view and then implement new actions, or reprioritize, with the new circumstances in place.

As managers and leaders of change, we need to anticipate change, anticipate resistance, breathe, lead and manage our people through the change: it's about people, not rocket science.

A CHECKLIST FOR LEADING PEOPLE THROUGH CHANGE

1. Create the vision for change.

2. Identify how different that vision is to the current vision.

3. Utilize holistic leadership by considering the whole person.

4. Define the type of change.

5. Identify the purpose or root cause of the change.

6. Use the organizational development approach to bottom it out.

7. Follow the ABChange model

8. Ask yourself, 'What does this mean to me?'

9. Expect resistance and be ready for it.

10. Breathe and lead through the change – it's a journey and/or a story about people!

CASE STUDIES

A number of case studies have already been shared throughout the book. However, I want to share how the ABChange model has impacted changes in a range of industries. These case studies are categorized, where possible, by the type of change and the industry in which the change occurred. This chapter should help you gain an even greater understanding of how you can lead your specific change by learning how others have led and managed change, quite possibly in your own industry or with regard to the same type of change.

WORKPLACE CHANGE

Case Study 1: A technology company

BACKGROUND

A technology company wanted to pilot agile working, with the aim of implementing it in a new building that was under construction at the time. It was crucial a team whose workload and working styles represented the majority of the workforce was identified, in order to build a business case for agile working to become a norm for the whole organization. Previously there had not been any significant workplace change within the organization, so there was no precedent for agile working. The culture was that every employee had their own desk, regardless of the level of utilization within the workspace overall.

There were a number of issues identified:

- Time: it was a six-week programme from start to finish.
- Utilization levels: these fluctuated greatly, ranging from very few people being in the office to everyone being required on a particular day, quarterly.
- Siloed working: people and teams worked in silos within and across teams, due to allocation of desks and little movement in the space.

The team wanted to achieve some clear objectives, including increasing collaboration, staff satisfaction (by adding value to coming into the office) and performance.

SOLUTION

Prior to commencement, there were two weeks of strong leadership coaching to obtain full commitment and responsibility. Due to the tight timescales, this was even more critical to acquire prior to starting the programme. The project itself was a complex change where there were two types of changes happening simultaneously for different groups. For example, the business and project leaders needed to build consensus, and hence a democratic leadership style was required in order to obtain buy-in to the change and new ways of working. This meant that they ensured key influencing groups and individuals were identified and actively involved in the delivery of the change. At the same time, the change champions (who were the influencing individuals and leaders within different teams) needed to get high performance from motivated teams. This required a pace-setting leadership style that involved the champions' role-modelling the behaviours once they were in the new space, but also inviting others to follow their lead. The champions also decided, during the preparation for the move, not to take a dictatorial style, but to lead by example and use a coaching style, which encouraged others to choose to demonstrate the right behaviours in the different spaces. This was manifested by posing an overarching question, 'Are you in the best space for your activity?', with two follow-up questions that applied to that specific space. For example, if a person was in a project table space, the follow-up questions were:

- Are you working across teams and interacting with colleagues?
- Do you need to share a screen with your colleagues to work on a common goal?

If the answer was 'yes' to both these questions, then the individual would know they were in the right space. However, if the answer was 'no', then they were not in the right space, thus creating a potential peer-pressure moment to move to a space better suited to the activity they were undertaking. This gave full accountability, responsibility and ownership to the individual (with some use of peer pressure) to use the spaces correctly.

IMPACT

Utilizing strong leadership styles and engagement that were appropriate to the different changes happening within the project for the business enabled a fairly seamless transition during the construction phase and at the time of the launch (as well as afterwards). There was a great deal of enthusiasm, anticipation and excitement built up using the different tactics defined in the ABChange model, across all the teams involved with the change. As a result, the time for the business to adapt to a new 'business as usual' model was immediate, with an increase in staff satisfaction of 146 per cent. Furthermore, there was clear evidence of cross-collaboration between teams, which was documented anecdotally.

Case Study 2: A technology company, continued, with a different team

BACKGROUND

Due to the success of the change outlined in Case Study 1, it was decided that this new way of working and design would be implemented across the business unit globally. There was a great deal of envy and desire to prove equality of flexibility in leadership and workplace styles. The team in Paris struggled to conduct business in a modern way due to a lack of technology capability and a modern environment, so the desire to change this was strong.

SOLUTION

A project team was put in place, and a cultural analysis was conducted, to understand any differences that may need to be taken into consideration. It was agreed, with the support of the local HR manager, that the work council needed to be initially engaged to help ensure buy-in and support for the change. The democratic leadership style was used and the work council were fully supportive of the change to happen; in fact, they were really quite enthusiastic for the change, as they recognized it as a way to create a showcase locally that their peers would be proud of and want to 'show off' to clients. Unfortunately, the senior leaders of the teams impacted did not have the self-confidence required to deliver the behavioural change at time of engagement, nor did they instil trust in the staff and work council that they would also adopt the change themselves. Instead, they focused more on working independently and creating rewards for the achieving work targets rather than the change. This meant they focused on the least important skills required to make this change, rather than the most important.

IMPACT

The enthusiasm and commitment from the work council and staff faded quickly, and individuals became cynical that the change would actually happen. In the end, the change did happen, but it was delayed for nearly a year, costing a great deal financially and emotionally and having detrimental impacts on the performance of the team.

Case Study 3: A media company

BACKGROUND

Workplace change projects for a media company had been previously focused on the logistics of the move. With the implementation of agile working, leaders needed to focus on the people side of the change. The purpose of the change was to build a new home that was a truly inspiring place to work, designed for flexibility and the future. There were three aims:

- To work together in new ways: a single site leading to more sharing and mixing of ideas.
- To be more flexible in order to achieve more: a fit-for-purpose place to work that makes better use of space, builds capacity and allows more achievement.
- To make it easier to get things done: new ways of working that will help to respond better to customers' needs.

To achieve this, the leadership team wanted to implement a ratio of 1:1.4 desks per person across an entire floor of an existing building, which would accommodate 300 people. There were several key issues:

- Staff has pride in the personalization of their space.
- There was already strong team collaboration and a perception this would decrease as a result of the change.

- A need to change the mindset of management that this was culture change and not just an office move.
- The management team did not have the skills to deliver the journey of change to their teams.

Aside from the change itself, culturally there was a great deal of competition across the teams, thus generating a level of discourse that needed to be managed with the change.

SOLUTION

A workshop was developed and delivered to the management team to help clarify and justify the level of change of the project and help build their change leadership skills. Through this workshop, the change coach or manager identified the change as a need to heal discourse due to the cultural drivers and aims of the business. Managers were required to utilize an affiliative leadership style, meaning they had to engage from an emotional perspective with how the change would impact their teams. They also needed to build on cross-team collaborations to help create more of a 'one team' alliance.

IMPACT

The strong engagement and cross-team participation was not only encouraged but also role-modelled by the management team. This significantly helped build the trust and collaboration required for healing the discourse. As a result, the teams fully engaged and participated in the change activities at a high level, including cross-team surveys, voting, workspace exhibitions and workshops. This meant a return to 'business as usual' with the new way of working occurred within a relatively short period of time (three weeks).

Case Study 4: A financial services organization

BACKGROUND

Workplace change projects for a financial sector organization had previously been focused on technology and processes and not on the people. However, the leadership team needed to implement agile working on a large scale across several building and business areas in various parts of the UK. Specifically, 7,000 staff in London and Sheffield needed to be converted to agile working, saving in excess of 800 workstations, and equating to £8.4 million of savings over a three-year period. The primary objective was to deliver a total floor space saving of twenty per cent with a 1:1.25 desk-sharing ratio. There were five key issues:

- Leadership needed to help enable staff to realize that work is something you do, not somewhere you go.

- The mindset for delivering change needed to switch from IT to people.
- A comprehensive change programme needed to be delivered on multiple sites.
- Managers did not have the management or change skills to deliver the change.
- Different supporting business areas needed to help deliver project outcomes that were outside 'business as usual' for them.

SOLUTION

The overall change was obtaining a high performance from a motivated team, which required a pace-setting leadership style. The difficulty with this leadership style is that it can become destructive if used over prolonged periods of time. However, the programme duration was twelve weeks, so there were no detrimental or potentially detrimental impacts. Focusing on people development rather than IT was key, while recognizing the three components (people, technology and new space) that were required for delivery. Firstly, the managers role-modelled and promoted the change with senior team members. They also developed a bespoke management charter and were visible at several social events to increase excitement. Multiple methods of communication (such as newsletters, drop-in sessions, workshops, etc.) that involved the senses of touch, sound and sight also helped ensure people had the right support and tools to deliver the change.

IMPACT

The company became more joined-up through flexible, progressive work environments that increased employee mobility, productivity and engagement. The business also benefitted from cost savings, as well as options for how and where people worked. The change balanced business, team and individual needs, and teams were provided with appropriate training, technology and support. There was improved employee engagement; better work-life balance; a focus on deliverables not presenteeism; increased trust; and reduced environmental impact. The initial achievement of the sustainable change occurred in a relatively short period of time of one week to reach 'new business as usual'.

Case Study 5: A telecommunications company

BACKGROUND

Workplace change projects at a telecommunications company had previously been implemented as local real-estate projects and had not focused on the people they impacted, much less ensured there were the support mechanisms in place (i.e., policies, processes and technology). The major challenge had been the lack of alignment of these change project with wider business culture change programmes. The organization had a strong culture and had also merged with another organization with a strong culture three years previously. The leadership team wanted to use a new workplace change project as a way of creating one culture throughout the organization, including creating new ways of working. There were multiple key challenges:

- The change project was not aligned with the wider organizational attributes (i.e., behaviour, values, performance management, other change programmes).
- The change was not seen as the driver for workplace change.
- The team impacted were siloed within the organization.
- The hierarchical culture of the organization made it difficult to manage change.
- Tailored training on the new way of working was needed for managers and staff.
- There were no clearly defined roles and responsibilities (including champions, project team, business managers and employees).
- There was no clear communication project timeline and plan.

SOLUTION

Even though at first glance this project seemed like an improvement or high-performance type of change, it was actually a building-consensus change because at its roots, it needed multiple people, from multiple disciplines and historically different organizations to come together and agree a way forward. This resulted in a democratic leadership style, which required strong governance of the different stakeholders, while giving them a clear opportunity to contribute at each stage of the change. The multiple culture programmes were then aligned and framed with an overarching change to help drive the smaller changes within the organization. This enabled staff within the organization to feel like one change was being implemented with the aim of adoption, rather than multiple different changes. This also helped reduce change fatigue, which was a potential risk within the organization. The change capability was also built with the leaders and managers within the organization to help them take a people and behavioural approach to the culture changes, giving staff the support they required.

IMPACT

By utilizing this approach and addressing change with a people focus, the change was coordinated and integrated into the organization. This enabled staff to feel they had the right support to make the behavioural changes required and ensured the organization had all the right mechanisms in place to prepare for and adopt the changes. This enabled the organization to create the feeling of 'one company' that helped drive the vision and performance of the organization overall.

Case Study 6: An insurance company

BACKGROUND

A global insurance company wanted to create an efficient workplace where innovation was a habit, collaboration was natural, effectiveness was embedded and their employees thrived, while reducing the cost base on real estate for the organization. They also wanted to create a showcase for their clients, and attract and retain talent. Some of the key challenges were the shape of the building and a culture of giving offices to individuals once they had reached a certain level, which was traditional across the industry. The company were looking to reduce the number of floors occupied in the building by three, with the aim of spreading the workforce more evenly across all the floors – thus reducing noise levels and overcrowding in some teams and increasing noise levels and interaction within other teams.

There was also a great mismatch between the size of the meeting rooms and the size of the meetings taking place. There were several further key issues:

- Staff were not fully bought into the change.
- Staff felt that the change was just a cost-cutting exercise and that executives and senior leaders would be exempt.
- Historically there had been attempts to implement the same change but it had not worked.

- There were concerns over finding available desks and locating colleagues; time wasted setting up; hygiene; and losing personal space.
- There were distinct cultures and working styles between different teams.

SOLUTION

It was critically important that this project took an immediate people-focused approach to help with the attitudes toward this change based on historic organizational events and the low staff motivation levels, if there was to be any chance of success. This meant that building consensus and a democratic leadership style was going to be required to enable delivery. Interviews with senior leaders and staff focus groups were conducted, in order to obtain a full picture of the situation. Interestingly, surveys were also delivered to all staff, but the results did not reflect the outcomes of the focus groups or interviews. This highlighted a potential underlying distrust across the teams and potentially within management.

Bearing all this in mind, a change network was established to ensure different teams were involved throughout the project. These teams were given, at times, autonomy to make decisions and the ability to influence the outcomes. When establishing the network, firstly, volunteers were requested and clear parameters and responsibilities were outlined to ensure participation would remain at a high level throughout the project timeline. The change network was promoted internally. This meant not only that staff knew who their representative was and who they could contact with questions, but also that individuals and the network had a higher profile within the organization. This generated a level of pride, responsibility and trust. The democratic leadership style was promoted through the training and the approach to the change network, thus ensuring the right impact would be achieved.

IMPACT

Taking the approach of building consensus and utilizing the steps outlined in the ABChange model meant that the key challenges outlined above were addressed. The staff were involved in helping define and design the workspace, by choosing names and particular pieces of furniture with the help of showcases and drop-in centres. The organization was able to reduce their footprint by three floors, while maintaining a sensitivity to the different working styles and needs of different teams.

Case Study 7: A telecommunications company

BACKGROUND

A telecommunications company was embarking on a great deal of cultural change driven by a shift in how the staff worked to complete tasks. Historically, real-estate changes were not people-focused, which meant leaders were failing to lead by example or would not buy into the new environment. They strongly encouraged traditional face-to-face cultures, and created confusion over flexible work arrangements, not helped by insufficient information about project expectations.

Statistics about the company highlighted some key issues:

- Forty-six per cent of seats went unused daily, on average.
- Eighty-nine per cent of employees spent time working remotely.
- Forty-seven per cent of collaborations were with employees in different time zones.
- Fifty-four per cent of employees described their work style as 'mobile'.

SOLUTION

Two changes were required at different levels of the organization: The leadership team needed to buy into the change and come to a consensus on the management of the new ways of working, requiring a democratic leadership style. This was demonstrated by obtaining executive support and sponsorship needed, with clear board approval. Formal communications from the leaders of the organization were distributed outlining the organization's key challenges and illustrating how the solution would address these. Clear roles and responsibilities were also outlined and put in place to ensure and demonstrate the full support and buy-in. Leaders (managers and directors) were fully engaged in practical exercises aimed at strengthening their effectiveness in leading a flexible workforce.

Staff were highly motivated, but a higher level of performance was needed, which could be achieved through a pace-setting leadership style. Once the leaders were on board, they were able to exemplify the new behaviours, clarify communication and expectations to staff. This was critical to be able to demonstrate to the staff that the leaders were setting examples of the new ways of working. The leadership teams needed to fully understand what the change was and how they needed to behave differently and then implement those new behaviours, which they did.

IMPACT

As a result of both changes (the leadership team building buy-in and consensus across the business, and the use of the pace-setting leadership style to exemplify the difference required in behaviour), staff were enabled to recognize what changes they needed to make and adopt those new ways of working.

TEAM COLLABORATION

Case Study 8: An infrastructure company

BACKGROUND

A team within the transportation business unit of an infrastructure company wanted to be able to describe to clients and partners how they worked in a collaborative way. This was driven by an industry change in how contracts would be assessed and commissioned going forward. The team was made up of long-serving civil engineers who were used to describing and communicating through the languages of processes and systems, rather than through behavioural language. They needed to change the language they used to describe their work and experiences, both in person for interviews and on paper for proposals.

SOLUTION

This was clearly an improvement change, because the team simply needed to change the way in which they communicated, and required a coaching leadership style. This was applied by creating a coaching programme that was divided up into three different elements to help the team and senior leaders involved:

1. Analysis: this looked at the way in which the team would write about their experiences and ways of working. They were then coached on how they could change the written language to illustrate more clearly their collaborative working style.
2. A workshop: this was designed and delivered to focus on team collaboration exercises. Once these exercises were completed, the team was asked to describe what and how the exercises unfolded. The facilitators coached the team in the language they would use to help illustrate the differences in using process language versus behavioural language.
3. Individual and group coaching: senior leaders received individual and a group sessions to help illustrate the changes they needed to make in how they communicated and also highlight the benefits this would have in other situations (i.e., performance management).

IMPACT

The team very much enjoyed the programme and learned a great deal. They started to use the new communication style in all the work they did. They also started to win several contracts that required the collaborative way of working to be illustrated, resulting in an increase in their revenue streams and a major impact on the organization's bottom line.

Case Study 9: A construction project (an architecture practice, an infrastructure company and a developer)

BACKGROUND

A large and publicly profiled construction project was being delivered through a collaboration between several companies. The difficulty came when the relationship between different teams within the companies started to break down, reducing both the level of collaboration and productivity. There were a range of key issues:

- There was a relationship breakdown between the architecture, development and project management teams.
- The level of trust was greatly reduced.
- Roles and responsibilities were not clear, generating a level of confusion and miscommunication.

SOLUTION

A workshop was developed to help rebuild the relationships across the different teams. A survey was also designed and implemented with the aim of highlighting the key areas that had the highest level of communication and team challenges. The change that was required was very much around healing discourse – the relationship between the teams was critical. It was paramount that the delivery team had the project team's full cooperation and buy-in for the design of the workshop, in order to obtain full ownership and responsibility for the outcomes of the workshop. As a result, the delivery team used an affiliative leadership style, which really helped ensure the teams were fully on board with the workshop. It was decided the best approach was for the workshop to take place on 'neutral territory', but in a local area, so that travel was minimized. The workshop then focused on the results of the survey, with the teams discussing the results generated and creating an action plan with agreed ways forward. Psychometrics were also utilized in the workshop to help illustrate key differences in preferred ways of communicating and how those might impact others.

IMPACT

Even though the team fully and correctly implemented the ABChange model and used the right leadership style throughout the workshop, tensions were still at a very high level and it took a great deal of affiliative leadership from the delivery team to keep things on an even keel. There were a few moments when tension was so high that unscheduled breaks were required to help the individuals in the teams diffuse some of their emotions.

This proves that even using the right methods and tactics can still sometimes not entirely eliminate emotions and tensions when trying to effect change. As leaders, we need to recognize the emotions of our teams and give them the space to be able to work through their emotions without isolation or criticism.

Case Study 10: A financial services organization

BACKGROUND

A financial services organization had been delivering a service at a high level, but several changes in the leadership team, along with changes to the organizational structure and team responsibilities, had created a good deal of confusion, frustration and anxiety. At the time, there was a great deal of change happening within the organization and staff were struggling to keep up with the pace of the change. There was a good deal of resistance for the change, which was seen as 'one more to deal with'. The change presented several key issues:

- There was a lack of clear leadership.
- There was no visibility between the teams and the key stakeholders.
- Leaders lacked the authority to follow up and address issues internally.
- There was a need to transfer knowledge within the teams and develop talent.

SOLUTION

A workshop was designed to not only share the results of a work assessment on the leaders from the different team's productivity, but to also review the relationships between the teams using psychometrics and team dynamics. The change required was very much around building consensus in order for them to recognize the key challenges, the impact they had on others and take responsibility for the outcomes of the workshop to make a difference. The leaders were required to demonstrate a democratic leadership style, which really came to the fore when one of the senior leaders was struggling to recognize how their preferred way of communicating impacted negatively on others. As a result, they talked about their own perception of this communication style, and how it might be perceived by others. Examples of this way of communicating were used on other team members, illustrating the impact it had on them. This information helped to highlight the effected leader's behaviours by focusing on what and how he could do things differently in a generic situation. Then, during a reflection exercise, the leader was able to illustrate more specifically how he can do things differently to produce different results, while using the ideas and learning from the peer discussions.

IMPACT

Approaching the change as one aimed at building consensus and using a democratic leadership style enabled the individuals to understand how things could be perceived by others, rightly or wrongly, and what they could do, as a result, differently. This really opened up conversations and increased the level of trust and honesty, so leadership team were able to come up with realistic solutions to the work performance issues.

Case Study 11: An infrastructure conglomerate

BACKGROUND

An infrastructure conglomerate was made up of two companies: an infrastructure company and a construction company. The two organizations were working together to build a new junction along a major roadway. The challenges were the organizations were approaching the project from different perspectives and they each had strong cultures that were not always aligned. The leadership team wanted to ensure there was strong collaboration across the whole team, regardless of which company a member happened to be employed by. The key objectives were to enable the project team to obtain high performance from a highly motivated team, and use effective communication skills to generate concise and efficient ways of working. There were several key issues:

- The leadership team avoided talking about things that might trigger conflict.
- Individuals felt pressured to agree and come to a consensus even though they might disagree.
- During meetings, individuals would become defensive when challenged.
- The leadership team was too polite to have real, open and honest conversations.

SOLUTION

This change was very much focused on obtaining high performance from already motivated teams, thus requiring a pace-setting leadership style, with the most important change skill being self-confidence from the delivery team. (The solution was implemented for a total of two weeks, so using the pace-setting style was not an issue.) Using the pace-setting style was paramount as both of the project teams were composed of civil engineers, whose natural approach to anything was to question and challenge and want proof that 'x' works before deploying. In order to help assess the change dynamics, each team member had to complete a survey that generated a set of results for the whole team. No individual results were compiled or shared – this meant the whole team would have to take responsibility for all the results and not blame, shame or criticize any particular individual. Also, because each individual contributed to the results, the results themselves could not be challenged as being subjective, as they were numerically based and presented. At each stage, the delivery team needed to demonstrate self-confidence in order to address specific challenges from the team – particularly when in a key area the results would show that only one or two individuals scored the question differently to the others. Some of the team members wanted to dismiss this result, but the project team challenged that it still meant that someone felt differently, so a new approach should be put forward. As a result the discussion was had, rather than dismissed.

IMPACT

Utilizing the ABChange model correctly in this situation was critical – it would have been easy to allow the senior leaders within the teams to 'take over' and dismiss some key conversations. The delivery team's self-confidence to ensure the method was the right way forward maximized the opportunity for those difficult conversations to actually take place rather than be swept under the carpet in the usual way. Afterwards, the team implemented the agreed actions, and had a much more honest conversation with everyone taking part, and the performance of the team increased as a result.

LEADERSHIP

Case Study 12: Central government

BACKGROUND

Charlotte, a senior civil servant was required to merge two teams to create a new function within the organization. The team members came from two very different parts of government and related to the function very differently (i.e., one group was more project focused and the other group took a more organizational approach). A great deal of friction had built up within the team and Charlotte realized she needed some help in trying to resolve the team issues and getting them to work together better and more collaboratively. She faced several difficulties:

- There were several different changes that needed to happen (e.g., conflict resolution).
- Decisions needed to be made about how to align the different business methods in each team, while preserving the best elements of both and holding a vision of the desired outcome for the organisation.
- There were two different teams with different histories and different needs

- There was a lot of conflict and difference in approaches, with individuals working in silos.
- Some members of the teams would be losing their jobs as part of the merger.
- Relocation for some team members would be part of the process.

SOLUTION

The coach worked with Charlotte using the ABChange model and identified she needed to heal discourse with team members. She realized she needed to use an affiliative leadership style, which she defined to mean that she had to meet with the individuals in the team on a one-to-one basis. She decided to ask them what they wanted from her and from the team – and not 'fill the silence' by trying to answer the question or ask more questions (her usual style); she had to wait and listen for their answer. One of her team members was so taken aback with the new approach, they ignored the question. When Charlotte raised this in a coaching session, the coach said that she needed to simply ask the question again, wait again for the answer and not let the individual ignore it. This would help build trust with the team member.

IMPACT

As a result of all this, Charlotte's confidence grew, as she realized she did not need to know all the answers – and by not giving solutions to all the problems she enabled team members to solve the problems themselves. This also generated more collaboration in her team because they suddenly had to go to their colleagues for help with solving issues, rather than go to Charlotte. Before, Charlotte had concentrated so much energy on getting things done, she ended up not managing the change of her new team effectively. By changing the focus and using the ABChange model in the coaching session, Charlotte made a great deal of progress with her team, which culminated in their ability to work together more cohesively and collaboratively, rather than working in silos.

Case Study 13: Central government

BACKGROUND

An organization based in central government had an internal reputation for avoiding 'difficult conversations' when it came to performance management. Managers and directors would typically opt to move staff to different areas of the organization, which only moved 'problems' around.

Furthermore, there was a great need or desire for the organization to align itself to the wider civil service in general. Therefore, a review of talent management, what behaviours constitute leadership and how leadership was measured needed to be considered, along with current government views on priorities.

- Senior management performance did not have a rigorous assessment process and talent management was perceived as an annual re-numeracy bonus, delivered based on 'favouritism'.
- Due to the sensitivities of managing performance, many times the unions would be involved in individual cases, which had a high risk of publicity.
- There was a need to change the hearts and minds of managers and directors with regard to the benefits and priorities of managing performance effectively.
- Staff needed to be equipped with the skills to have difficult conversations and familiarized with new processes on short timescales.
- Board agreement was needed to align the leadership behaviours and skills with the wider civil-service framework. Many of the board members had helped create the current organizational leadership vision or behaviours.

SOLUTION

This change was very much about improvement, and required a coaching leadership style. The system was not necessarily 'broken' – it just needed to be aligned and managed more effectively. A process was created in collaboration with wider civil-service learning networks that included a comprehensive development programme for identified talent. This generated incentive for the managers to be involved, as it would progress their careers and open opportunities that were previously unavailable to them. The civil-service framework was also mapped directly on to the organization's leadership framework, demonstrating to the board the similarities in the frameworks (just a difference in language), which enabled them to easily adopt the 'new' approach. A series of workshops were also rolled out to all managers and directors to ensure they all had the knowledge and skills to implement the new process into the immediate and existing timescales, to reduce disruption to workloads and work cycles. Furthermore, there were monitoring groups established to ensure consistency of application and messaging.

IMPACT

Using a coaching leadership style helped build the confidence of managers to implement the change effectively, but most importantly to them, objectively. They wanted to ensure they could carry out constructive conversations with the aim of improving individuals. They were able to do this by asking questions and allowing their staff to generate the answers, rather than feel they had to create the answers and either criticize or praise the individual. A clear definition of what constitutes leadership within the organization was established and measured, and clear development plans were implemented for managers that previously did not exist. There was full participation from the managers and directors, leading to more effective management of performance, and timescales were met by all 220 members. All budget constraints and restrictions were met within time of the existing organizational work cycles.

Case Study 14: An infrastructure project organization

BACKGROUND

An organization owned by a consortium of investors was helping to deliver a large infrastructure project. There were multiple sites divided up into regions, with a project sponsor responsible for the different regions and the deliverables within that area, including project deliverables and community relationship deliverables. There was a need to change the role of the project sponsors and the focus of the organization from planning to delivering a significant infrastructure project. While systems, processes and capability had evolved over a prolonged period during project feasibility and design development, the step-change to delivery needed to be sudden and resolute. There were a range of key issues:

- The project involved multiple stakeholders, each with a different set of priorities.
- There was a large team to manage, made up of people from different organizations creating a matrix environment.

- Roles and responsibilities were not clearly defined across all the teams.
- Financial and resource management were complex.
- IT and some processes were developed, but the scope of the people side of change was not fully recognized.

SOLUTION

The change required obtaining buy-in and consensus from the varying stakeholders, but it was managed as a healing discourse change, which sent the leader down a different path. Instead of using a democratic leadership style, the leader focused on an affiliative leadership style. The main difference being the leader focused on the emotions of the different individuals and stakeholders involved and understanding the situation from their perspective. Although an element of this was required, a more democratic style in which their points of view and ideas on how to create solutions for themselves could have been more productive and successful. The main difference this generated was that the leader ended up working more on their own, in an individual capacity, to 'come up with the answers or resolve the issues' rather than involving the team in doing this themselves. This slightly different focus with regard to prioritizing change skills had a real impact on the outcomes of the change.

IMPACT

Difficult decisions were tackled directly; some resources, systems and functionality were no longer needed, while establishing new capabilities needed to be managed and integrated into the business change. However there were areas where this was not successful and mistakes were made. Fortunately, to help with this, a continuous improvement and feedback loop was established, which helped the team to adjust and modify their approach. Optimism bias resulted in an underestimation of the duration of the transition period. This was possibly down to the different focus on working independently, as there is a tendency to underestimate the amount of time things will take when we work more on our own. As a result, adjustments were required to recognize the change was really about culture and behaviours, not commodities, and some expectations had to be realigned. In the end, the change happened, but it was a bit more painful than it would have been, had it been recognized as the right type of change at the start.

Case Study 15: Central government

BACKGROUND

An agency within central government had a culture of autocratic management. Coaching was viewed as a specific management tool, only to be used in specific development situations. It was not seen as a tool to be used quickly in order to create an effective and efficient way of managing teams and stakeholders. Nor was it embedded into any of the agency's people processes and systems.

Furthermore, the agency went through a merger and acquisition within a central government department, which transformed the structures of the organization and required several processes and systems to be reviewed for the future development of the agency.

- High retention rates were present within management grades creating a top-heavy organization.
- Some organizational processes and systems were no longer 'fit for purpose'.
- The organization was not prepared for the future level of work with the current staff levels under the existing management culture.
- The organization was growing rapidly and needed to be able to upskill and develop staff quickly.
- The organization was required to create a new product that required a new way of working internally and externally.

SOLUTION

A new function was created in the human-resources department of the agency that focused on leadership and management development. One of the primary objectives of the function was to create a coaching culture in order to meet the new demands on the business and enable managers to develop their people more effectively, thus creating an improving change.

A coaching programme was designed with the aim of creating a coaching culture within the agency within three years. Clear objectives and deliverables were identified and agreement was reached with senior managers and the board by using a coaching leadership style. Key questions were put forward to help the executives recognize that creating of a coaching culture was key to be able to deliver the organization's objectives.

The programme was designed to target different levels of skill and capability based on the different requirements of the business. First, an educational campaign was launched about elements of coaching. Knowledge was leveraged based on previous leadership programmes, in which all managers across the organization participated.

Second, a short workshop session was developed to give managers an opportunity to practise their coaching skills in a safe environment, recognizing that coaching can be used to achieve quick wins and does not just have to involve one-hour development sessions. A digital coaching forum was created for managers to share experiences and gain insights from peers and colleagues on coaching. A leadership blog was established to share success stories across the organization.

Third, an accredited coaching programme was implemented and linked to the International Coaching Federation, all of which contributed to building the coaching capability across multiple levels. This enabled the organization to develop an internal network of qualified coaches to be used for key organizational systems and processes (i.e., outplacement, talent management and performance management). The qualified coaches volunteered to participate but had to go through a full assessment that required the commitment of their managers and directors, as time out from their normal working responsibilities would be necessary.

Fourth, networks were created within the agency, at a cross-departmental level and at a cross-governmental level, to enable managers and trained coaches to share learning and experiences and raise their profiles.

IMPACT

Utilizing the coaching leadership style throughout the improvement change really helped educate and bring the whole organization, at multiple management levels, along on the journey over the years of implementation and eventually adoption. Investors in People (IiP) evaluated that a coaching culture was in existence and thriving across the entire organization ahead of schedule, within eighteen months.

- Forty-six staff members and managers received qualifications through the accreditation programme within two years.
- Talent was seen as being more thoroughly developed within the organization and managers were exposed to other areas of government.
- Performance management conflicts were reduced.
- The coaching culture is seen by the agency as a success and still exists.

CULTURE CHANGE

Case Study 16: Central government

BACKGROUND

Due to a change in government, a central agency needed to undergo a number of transformational changes that included creating a new customer network, shutting down a regional office and refocusing the products and services the agency offered. Redundancy was not something that typically occurred at this point in central government, therefore the organization was not ready to deal with the people issues.

- There was so much information, leaders did not know what the first steps were.
- Changes were happening to lots of people in different capacities in offices across the UK.
- Line managers and senior managers were not always in control of the changes.
- Leaders needed to be able to plan and manage the people through the change effectively.

SOLUTION

This change was about healing discourse, as redundancy was (and still is for many) an emotionally challenging time for those that were made redundant and those that were 'left behind'. As a result, this required an affiliative leadership style with a real focus on building the trust of all those involved, having the self-confidence to have difficult conversations and collaborate with a number of support teams to enable the actions required in a sensitive manner. This was demonstrated by understanding the perspectives of the key stakeholder groups – surplus or redundant staff, line managers of surplus or redundant staff and leaders managing organizational change – and putting three main activities in place to support them.

Virtual space was created: a web page brought together all the opportunities in one place: job searches, practical support, emotional support and MyNetwork, which was an internal networking tool for staff.

Physical space was created, to help people through the transition, in the form of an outplacement centre: this space hosted training and networking events, seven laptops with easy external access and a training room. Executive staff participated in and endorsed training and events.

A senior development programme was implemented: managers were encouraged to develop the change skills to lead people through change, whether that was for redeployment or redundancy. The focus was on generating change through a collaborative approach with staff, stakeholder mapping and analysis and managing resistance.

IMPACT

People felt they were taken care of during a major transition for the organization. They understood the opportunities available to them. The level of dissatisfaction with the process of redundancy or redeployment was decreased, as messages were more clearly communicated to the staff affected and they received the required amount of support. They felt their wellbeing was a high priority for the organization because senior management participated in running key workshops for the affected staff at the outplacement centre.

Case Study 17: A health technology organization

BACKGROUND

A leading health technology company was focused on improving people's health and enabling better outcomes in prevention, diagnosis, treatment and home care. They used advanced technology and deep clinical and consumer insights to deliver integrated solutions. In order to increase efficiencies within the support areas of the organization, it was decided to move a function from Europe to India. In order to achieve this, recruitment and training was required to minimize the risk of losing valuable organizational process and systems information and ensure the smooth transition of the functional requirements.

Once the decision had been made, the development of the new team happened almost immediately, requiring an intense on-boarding programme lasting four weeks for each cohort to be designed at speed (there were two cohorts). The design phase started two weeks prior to the delivery stage.

There were a range of challenges:

- On-boarding needed to be developed without full knowledge of the capability of the audience.
- Training needed to be developed in one week and delivered the following week.
- Training was developed in the UK and delivered in India by a local trainer.

- The trainer needed to be trained virtually to ensure understanding and effective delivery.
- Due to commercial reasons, some tools could not be used, so new tools had to be created.
- The virtual team had not worked together before and were geographically spread across the globe (in the UK, Europe and India).
- Training needed to be highly engaging in order to inspire and excite new members of staff, while giving them the technical tools to complete the tasks.

SOLUTION

The change was definitely a building consensus and buy-in type of change because it was critical for all involved to be fully agreed and bought into the process, tools and tactics used to develop and deliver the on-boarding programme. Thus a democratic leadership style was required and utilized to help bring the team together and ensure they were all involved in each step, with defined roles and responsibilities in order to ensure the delivery could happen within the extraordinarily tight timelines. A huge amount of trust had to be established immediately across a virtual team. This was achieved by setting definitive agreed actions and plans with clear deadlines, which were met every step of the way. If a deadline was delayed or there was a barrier potentially resulting in a delay, it was communicated immediately with everyone involved to help unblock. A regular weekly time was set up to conduct the train-the-trainer sessions, with an additional day set aside for any follow-up questions or issues that needed to be addressed before delivery the following working day.

IMPACT

The programme was delivered with resounding success. The participants were fully engaged in the activities and satisfaction scores were very high. The virtual team, although exhausted, were exhilarated with the energy and collaboration that was demonstrated throughout the whole project. Identifying the right type of change and using the right leadership style with the focus on the most important change skills – particularly, in this case, building trust – was absolutely critical in achieving this success.

Case Study 18: A clinical commissioning group

BACKGROUND

A clinical commissioning group (CCG) was carrying out four primary workstreams. Each of these workstreams were being carried out independently and without a clear umbrella message. The primary purpose of the CCG was to demonstrably improve the quality, nature and extent of services in the area. In order to help accomplish this, a central message on the different workstreams needed to be fully developed to help demonstrate a more joined-up service.

The ramifications of not having a refined overarching message clearly articulated meant the benefits of the CCG were unclear and unconcise.

The CCG was slightly different culturally to neighbouring CCGs, because it was clinically lead with management input, rather than the other way round. There were approximately forty to fifty staff members (including the governing body), at the time. The staff surveys demonstrated a content and hard-working staff with very high satisfaction results. There were a number of regular meetings across the different reporting levels within the organization with a full governing body that consists of general practitioners, consultants, nurses, senior management and public-health representatives.

There was, at the time, a vision and aims set for the organization to follow, however there was a question regarding the potential relevance of these aims.

SOLUTION

The leadership team needed to create a change strategy that enabled the organization to articulate clearly and concisely what its vision meant and what benefits it would deliver to their stakeholders.

An overarching message needed to be established so all the current and future workstreams and projects could easily be connected to the business objectives. This message would need to be easily adapted by all the practices and the stakeholders, so there was a clear understanding of the relevance of the workstreams in relation to the vision and aims of the organization.

The message needed to define a framework that drove the activities of the organization. This was a realignment for the organization that brought focus onto the activities that were already being delivered. Therefore, the staff should not feel a large organizational change had taken place – just a refocused, concise and clear message articulated that helped them define what they were doing and why.

This change was clearly aimed at building consensus, as it required all the different stakeholder groups to come to an agreed understanding and to buy into the new vision to help deliver a service fit for purpose. Therefore a democratic leadership style was required by the leaders of the organization to help obtain this consensus and buy-in. They worked closely with the different stakeholder groups and ensured each of the different groups were involved in developing the strategy through interviews and focus groups conducted by a third party. An analysis was then drafted and a framework created that generated a visual to illustrate an inclusive approach, which was fundamental to the CCG's ethos and methodology.

IMPACT

By identifying the correct change type and using the ABChange model correctly, the CCG was able to implement and adopt a framework whereby all the stakeholders felt they had involvement in creating, thus generating a consensus of the strategy and focus for adoption. This also helped establish a collaborative approach among the stakeholders that was then easily used to solve key operational challenges going forward.

REFERENCES

Argyris, C. (1985) *Strategy, Change and Defensive Routines*, Boston: Pitman Publishing Ltd.

Bennett, R. (1997) *Organizational Behaviour*, 3rd edn, London: Pearson Professional Ltd.

Beer, M., Eisenstat, R. A., and Spector, B. (1990) *The Critical Path to Corporate Renewal*, Cambridge: Harvard Business School Press.

Barends, E. Briner, R., Mawson, A., Plum, K., Rousseau, D. (2014) *The Six Factors of Knowledge Worker That Changed Everything*, London: Advanced Workplace Associates. https://www.advanced-workplace.com/wp-content/uploads/2015/04/AWA-6-factors-of-knowledge-worker-productivity-2.pdf

Bryan, J. (2009) *How Leadership Skills Impact Organizational Change*, London: City University MSc dissertation.

(2014) *Journey of Leadership in the Workplace*, London: Wolters Kluwer Ltd.

(2018) Successfully Managing Change in the Workplace, *Corporate Real Estate Journal* vol. 8.1 (Oct–Nov 2018): Henry-Stuart Publications, pp. 1–12.

Burnes, B. (2004) *Managing Change: A Strategic Approach to Organizational Dynamics (Fourth Edition)*, Harlow: Prentice Hall.

Creasey, T., and Hiatt, J. (2012) *Change Management: The People Side of Change*, 2nd edn, Loveland: Prosci Inc.

Dawson, S. (1996) *Analysing Organisations*, *3rd* edn, London: MacMillan Business.

Dietz, G., and Den Hartog, D.N. (2006) Measuring Trust Inside Organisations, *Personnel Review* vol. 35 (5), pp 557–588. Online version also available at: http://www.emeraldinsight.com/journals.

Dunphy, D., and Stace, D. (1993) The Strategic Management of Corporate Change, *Human Relations* vol. 46, London: Tavistock Institute, pp. 905–920.

Festinger, L. (1954) A Theory of Social Comparison Processes, *Human Relations* vol. 7 (2), London: Tavistock Institute, pp. 117–140.

Fiedler, F.E. (1967) *A Theory of Leadership Effectiveness*, New York: McGraw-Hill Books Co.

Fullen, M. (2001) *Leading in a Culture of Change*, San Francisco: Jossey-Bass.

Gillen, N., and Jeffery, H. (2014) See, The Next Generation Occupier Issue 1: *Do Your Homework*, London: AECOM, p. 15.

Goleman, D. (2002) *The New Leaders: Transforming the Art of Leadership into the Science of Results*, London: Time Warner Books.

(2000) Leadership That Gets Results, *Harvard Business Review On Point* 4487 (March–April), pp. 78–91.

Hersey, P., and Blanchard, K.H. (1969) *The Management of Organizational Behaviour*, 3rd edn, New Jersey: Prentice Hall.

Juneja, P. (2018) Reviewed by Management Study Guide Content Team. In *Importance of Communication in Change Management*. managementstudyguide.com

Kanter, R.M. (1989) *When Giants Learn to Dance: Mastering the Challenge of Strategy, Management and Careers in the 1990s,* London: Simon and Schuster.

Katz, D., and Kahn, R.L. (1966) *The Social Psychology of Organizations*, New York: John Wiley and Sons.

Kotter, J.P. (1995) Leading Change: Why Transformation Efforts Fail, *Harvard Business Review* vol. 73, March–April 1995, pp. 59–67.

Kübler-Ross, E. (1969). *On Death and Dying: What the Dying Have to Teach Doctors, Nurses, Clergy and Their Own Families*, New York: Scribner.

Lewin, K. (1935) *A Dynamic Theory of Personality,* New York: McGraw-Hill.

Mabey, C., and Mayon-White, B. (1993) *Managing Change*, 2nd edn, London: Sage Publications.

Mawson, A. (2020) Remote Working: The Science Behind Managing Virtual Teams, *Forbes Magazine.* https://www.forbes.com/sites/amawson/2020/06/17/the-science-behind-managing-virtual-teams/#45e743e82023

McGill, I., and Brockbank, A. (2004) *The Action Learning Handbook*, London: Routledge Farmer.

Mendoza, M. (2014) Work, *Breaking Better* 1, London: Chartered Institute of Personnel Development, p. 24.

Mitchell, T., and Larson, J.R. (1989) *People in Organizations: An Introduction to Organizational Behaviour*, New York: McGraw-Hill Book Co.

Morgan, G. (1997) *Images of Organization*, London: Sage.

Nadler, D. A., and Tushman, M. L. (1979), A Congruence Model for Diagnosing Organizational Behavior. In *Organizational Psychology: A Book of Readings*, 3rd edn, ed. Kolb, D., Rubin, I. and McIntyre, J., Englewood Cliffs, NJ: Prentice-Hall.

Peters, T. (1991) *Thriving on Chaos: Handbook for a Management Revolution*, New York: Harper Collins.

Prosci (2018) *Best Practices in Change Management*, Prosci Benchmarking Report, 10th edn, Fort Collins: Prosci Inc.

Rogers, E. (1962) *Diffusion of Innovations*, New York: The Free Press (a division of Simon and Schuster).

Stebbins, S. (June 2017) *Change Management Methodology and Strategic Communication: An Essential Partnership*. https://www.forbes.com/sites/forbescoachescouncil/2017/06/19/change-management-methodology-and-strategic-communication-an-essential-partnership/#9290d417b32c

Treadwell, J.R., Lucas, S., and Tsou, A.Y. (2014) Surgical Checklists: A Systematic Review of Impacts and Implementation, *BMJ Quality and Safety*. http://qualitysafety.bmj.com/content/early/2014/01/16/bmjqs-2012-001797

ABOUT THE AUTHOR

Jennifer Bryan is a practising Change Consultant and published author, who has worked with over thirty different organizations across multiple industries. She is also a Non-Executive Board Member of the ACMP (Association of Change Management Professionals) UK Chapter. She believes in helping people – in whatever capacity she can – by making sure people are thought of first, last and throughout change projects and programmes. She has created a unique leading change framework, the ABChange Model, which is shared in this book along with multiple case studies when it has been used. The Model is underpinned by accepted theories in leadership and change. It then builds upon them a framework which enables managers to create their own strategies and action plans, effecting specific change within their organizations.

As well as this book, Jennifer is author to the articles 'Successfully Managing Change in the Workplace' in *Corporate Real Estate Journal* vol. 8 (1), 'Journey of Leadership in the Workplace' in *iCroner* (September 2014) and 'Lead Behaviour' in *Coaching at Work* (July 2012).

Made in the USA
Las Vegas, NV
22 August 2021

28476780R00094